STON PUBLIC LIBRARY

00793 6238

P

West, Paul, 1930-

A stroke of genius :
illness and
    c1995. FEB   1995

JAN 1 2 1995

A STROKE
OF GENIUS

A STROKE *of* GENIUS

Illness and Self-Discovery

PAUL WEST

VIKING

EVANSTON PUBLIC LIBRARY
1703 ORRINGTON AVENUE
EVANSTON, ILLINOIS 60201

VIKING
Published by the Penguin Group
Penguin Books USA Inc., 375 Hudson Street,
New York, New York 10014, U.S.A.
Penguin Books Ltd, 27 Wrights Lane,
London W8 5TZ, England
Penguin Books Australia Ltd, Ringwood,
Victoria, Australia
Penguin Books Canada Ltd, 10 Alcorn Avenue,
Toronto, Ontario, Canada M4V 3B2
Penguin Books (N.Z.) Ltd, 182–190 Wairau Road,
Auckland 10, New Zealand

Penguin Books Ltd, Registered Offices:
Harmondsworth, Middlesex, England

First published in 1995 by Viking Penguin,
a division of Penguin Books USA Inc.

1 3 5 7 9 10 8 6 4 2

Copyright © Paul West, 1995
All rights reserved

Portions of this book first appeared in *Harper's,*
The New York Times, TriQuarterly,
and *The Village Voice Literary Supplement.*

LIBRARY OF CONGRESS CATALOGING IN PUBLICATION DATA
West, Paul.
A stroke of genius: illness and self-discovery/Paul West.
p. cm.
ISBN 0–670–84956–1
1. West, Paul—Health. 2. Chronically ill—Biography.
3. Authors—Biography. I. Title.
RC108.W42 1995
362.1'96—dc20
[B]   94–20642

This book is printed on acid-free paper.

Printed in the United States of America
Set in Sabon
Designed by Ann Gold

Without limiting the rights under copyright
reserved above, no part of this publication
may be reproduced, stored in or introduced into
a retrieval system, or transmitted, in any form
or by any means (electronic, mechanical, photo-
copying, recording or otherwise), without the
prior written permission of both the copyright
owner and the above publisher of this book.

For
Diane Ackerman
and
Anis I. Obeid, M.D.

CONTENTS

A STROKE
OF GENIUS

OVERTURE

I

The rueful jubilation in what follows honors a trajectory, perhaps a crash dive, certainly a chronic illness whose phases have always puzzled me and some of my doctors. The weird constellation of my symptoms has something to it of infernal wizardry, and I still lack the synoptic holist of a doctor who can put it all together, dominating by naming it. Surely, I ruminate, so many things gone wrong over a long time do not necessarily belong together; they just overlap, far from being siblings. I wonder, though, if there are not invisible linkages, like those Vietnam bridges built under water. My artist's sense of symmetry craves relatedness and clear lines of causation, from hives and flesh tags to migraine and stroke, and thence to diabetes. Prey to miscellaneous degenerations, I want them to be an opera, say, or a fathomable tableau. As the reader will find, one ailment goes away just as another begins, but only because a drug for the latter happens to cure both; and I naturally wonder if this same drug, administered early, for the former, might have precluded the latter. I think so, and lament the untimeliness of treatment.

Resentment and anger figure here too, as my title intimates in its grudging tribute to disease's ingenuity and brilliance, catching me smug and off guard as it did, my mind on a quite different ailment. But you will find also an honorable bigotry, a perverse pride in what has ailed me, and goes on doing so. An illness faced down, transcended, or even talked to death, becomes a prized possession, first draft of a novel you cannot bear to destroy but keep by you to hearten and remind. An exuberance came with the euphoria of my continual migraines, whereas the feelings attaching to later troubles were closer to contemplative infatuation, the author dotingly become his own raw material, poring over symptoms with near-philatelical zeal. If we can steel ourselves to take the planetary or racial view of our own medical destinies, we may end up, as I think Sir Thomas Browne and Proust ended up, regarding disease as the supreme art form, carved into us with a free and sometimes languid hand, not always successful at first but in the long run a triumph, allowing us at the last a sigh of miserable envy or just an anthropocentric jeer. To be born is to be transmutable, for better or for worse, while awaiting the worst. While watching my body assume some of its final distortions, I have managed to do a great deal of work, not always in defiance, and I now and then think its stammering downfall has inspired me, which is to say animated me beyond the usual. I have to be grateful for the provocation in what has gone wrong, even for the enlightenment therein, awakening me to biological magic I would otherwise have never known about. The great thing is to have had the chance to say or write my say while ailing, unlike others, whose diseases have blotted out their intellects along with their bodies. For that relief, *muchas gracias*, fluke as it was. Deepest thanks go to those who have put up with me in my illnesses, from the near and dear to relatively impersonal nurses and doctors caught up in their own art (a kind of anti-art, really, if disease is art too). I have not been a model patient, being too much given to defying and denying, yet never in hope of being exempted, always with some piece of writing to be done at all costs. When obsession meets the incurable, creativity sprouts wings.

Cleaning a toilet seat with a wisp of paper can sometimes, because you have pressed too hard, yield a muffled squeak, much as a note can sometimes flow from the rim of a glass. That's what happens here. I press down too hard, as I was exhorted not to do in kindergarten; it grooves the page(s) beneath. For me, inevitably, the maladies of yesteryear figure as backdrop; I wrote about them retrospectively, not on the spot, whereas about later things I have written recently indeed, without having them quite in focus—

awaiting the next scene, the ensuing mishap. I hope
that, as the reader advances, the sections already read
will function as a similar backdrop, settling into the
essayistic and poised while later pieces have some ur-
gency, with the patient-author on the raw, blustering
and uncouth. The longer you survive something, the
more measured your prose about it becomes: the
more the blown rose will curl its lip; the more a hormone patch on a woman's waist will resemble a
transparent postmark; the more you will grin when
your editor tells you over the phone *she* has just written *you* and is right now licking your envelope. Some
of this book amounts to free-ranging *bavardage;*
some of it has made me feel awkward as a sea cow
in snowshoes.

II

The backdrop to all that happens here is a series of
migraine attacks beginning at age ten and continuing
at monthly intervals for some forty years, turning my
visual field into a wasteland of sizzling white flares,
giving me caustic headaches no aspirin could quell. It
was as if I were being softened up for something else,
and worse. At about thirty, having had enough, I decided to write an account of how the migraines felt,
what they were, and I ended up with an essay that
almost enacts the phenomena of migraine; if you
don't have it, this essay will just about graft it onto
you. That essay now appears as an appendix, rele-

gated there because, although it was the prelude to
other illnesses, it would slow the reader to a crawl,
miring him or her in a prose style—costive and
dense—I use only for special purposes, certainly not
for overtures. It remains a document of its time, best
left as it is because of its heaving indignation, its perverse thick euphoria. The reader is welcome to turn
to it now, to read it last, or to ignore it as a juvenile
aberration.

No wonder migraineurs feel a bond of sympathy with
epileptics, hysterics, and spastics; but our sense of being out of control, while being also undistortedly
aware of the fact from moment to moment, is one
thing they do not share. In ambivalent experience, we
come closer to sufferers from Parkinson's disease or
Huntington's chorea, and often (as sometimes before
a menu whose print swarms and veers, or trying to
obey a traffic light whose colors combine) look just
as unfit. Our lives are Möbius strips: the outside becomes the inside without much warning, and any
slight tilt in customary sensations—an enhanced relish, a quickening in repartee, a minimal intuition of
something extrasensory—can herald the roller-
coaster, wall-of-death vertigo of a full-blown attack:
one's visual field turns into a moiré effect of watered
or wavy patterns, which are the spectrum scrambled
(usually minus its greens) in slow motion, though
with certain brilliant nodes of light erupting like tiny

supernovae within the overall scheme. When I saw the spectacular light show in Stanley Kubrick's film *2001,* with astronaut Bowman hurtling through canyons of explosive, irregular color, I felt on familiar ground, or at least in home ether, and for thirty seconds or so quite ignored the chance of the display's triggering an attack (as a strobe light can), such is the visual cortex's vulnerability.

I grew up half subscribing to theories that chocolate was the villain in the piece but knowing full well I could almost guarantee an attack by staring at sunlit snow or brightly lit white paper (hazards while sledding or reading!). In later years, the ballistically perfect, unrelievedly dazzling walls of a squash court had much the same effect, so I played the game in dark glasses and thus now and then slung racquet at a ball that wasn't there; but this was still better, half-play in the half-light, than to invalid myself altogether under the blaze of the roof's bogus noon. Taken unawares, I have supermarketed, cooked, and lectured during attacks, never mind that the price tags danced in fragments, or that I could not see what I stirred while it bubbled or what roasted behind the newly opaque see-through panel in the oven door, or that whatever notes I had were useless and the audience had become a random collage of the physiognomies present. There was one examination I did not finish (I could see none of the questions entire) and only one cricket match when I failed to go in to bat (the billet of willow between my hands just would not appear when I looked for it).

Told of your trouble, people are usually sympathetic, although baffled and a touch suspicious. According to W. H. Auden, migraine haunts all who suppress their rage, whether or not causing them to hallucinate. According to others, it's the blight of the high-strung perfectionist (or even, I suppose, of the placid perfectionist or the neurasthenic stoic). According to me, migraine is rather democratic, afflicting plowmen, bankers, hurdlers, and academics in equal measure, although I have sometimes thought that those subject to it might form an exclusive league along the lines of the Caterpillar Club (for those who've parachuted from a plane, their emblem a silkworm), *our* emblem a halved head or the sliced eye from Buñuel's *Un Chien Andalou,* a movie I cannot watch without marveling at its decipherment of the migraineur's longing to pluck out the sloven half of the jelly that offends (except that it's the half-cranium that's to blame, not the eye at all).

One lives as prudently as one can, careful not to lock gazes with flashbulbs, headlights, or televisor's lamps, and to be on special guard against the brute magnesium spot that is sunlight bull's-eyed on the chrome trim of a car: a photon punch whose aftereffect swells in just a few minutes from a retinal black hole into a band of brightness that spreads across your vision like the charring scar on a newspaper held against the fireplace to increase the draft. Soon the paper blazes up, of course, whereas the eyes blank out in a spherical funk in which not even banner headlines can be read.

How does it go? ". . . A flash of light in his brain, and with exceptional impetus all his vital powers suddenly started working at high tension. The sense of being alive, of being self-aware, was multiplied tenfold in these moments, instants, which passed like flashes of lightning. His mind and heart were flooded with extraordinary light. . . ." *The Idiot,* the epileptic. Misquoted, of course. Something akin: I share the preliminary aura, but *I* get off lightly. O vigilant guardhouse of the brain stem, topped by those dynamo halls of drives and emotions under the vast roof of the cerebral cortex, why do you do us like you do? Very kindly, you stage the answer to yourself without passing it on, pose the question back to me with enigmatic servitude. You relay the message like a telephone without ever, it seems, having received it your it-self.

I smile at the self-conscious patly misquoting victim who gestures to himself while burning; who, in those days, found his life's bane in the queen of the senses, so called; who could not see, beyond the fascination of what's difficult, as Yeats called it, the bliss of what's impossible (meaning here what shouldn't happen to those pearls his eyes). It took him no little

time to muster, as I have described them here, the
lavish conjurations that exploit a neurophysical de-
fect. But the bit that ends the jotting ("It will soar
out of my mouth into the Milky Way around me")
still pleases while a more accommodated I relishes
analogies between what happens during a bout and,
say, the shredded silver foil dumped from the air in
World War II to mislead enemy radar, or the curious
truth that light can move a block of wood if you
reduce it to finest fluffy sawdust, thus giving the pressure of light the maximum surface to work upon, the
merest gravity to work against. A star of gall in one's
head is nothing to be envied, of course, but it has its
motley allure, conferring auspices that yield estimably
lurid half-alliances I am not now eager to wish away:
Saul, occasionally promised comets, and I, at our
own speeds, marking time while it marks us. Or King
Lear, pathetically misidentifying the blinded Glouces-
ter as Goneril with a white beard.

Such painful ecstasies I had. I grew more lyrical
about my migraines than I did about my eventual
stroke. The sufferer became more and more teed-off,
yet without quite losing his sense of being smothered
in the miraculous, even to the point of recognizing
that all that has happened to him—good and bad—
is his, never to be shrugged or commanded off. I have
become what I am, not in spite of what has happened
to me, but because of it. My etiology and I have become grudging allies. Unlike Lindbergh, who clipped

off his transatlantic maps the corners he wasn't going to need (if he was that bad a navigator, then just don't go), I keep pasting supplements to mine, conjectural treasure charts for some blithe journey as yet unclear.

It was only much later, in 1992, the year in which I write this, long after my migraines have gone, that I read in *Science News* about research done concerning people with a history of both severe depression and headaches accompanied by auras. If you are depressed, it seems, then migraines accompanied by tinnitus, nausea, blurred vision, or extreme sensitivity to light will boost your tendency to suicide. The auras are bad for your state of mind, whether you are depressed or not. I was never much depressed, though prone to rage. Oddly enough, euphoria often attends the onset of an attack and lasts for quite a while. I count myself lucky: In the Detroit study done by Naomi Breslau of Henry Ford Hospital, fourteen of twenty-six adults who suffered severe depression plus migraines with auras attempted suicide. Depressed enough, I would probably never have written this book or any other. The light show switched on in the Slough of Despond can get you to do away with yourself.

S E E I N G
S O T U Q N A N G U

*There was almost no weather but the sun, and it
was hard not to feel young, lucky, imperishable,
born to watch the sunsets forever, as they shifted
and wheeled, wan and flush, with sometimes a
horizontal spectrum above them ascending from red
to violet.*

The Shapelessness of Things to Come

Fingering and tasting some six hundred attacks re-
news for me the last two I had: prosaic enough figures
against a dazzling, dementing ground. The first was
a series of tiny ones, actually, all happening in my
apartment in Tucson in 1984, maybe because the
light of late spring was ferocious and I had formed
the habit of writing each morning in an eastward-
facing room that blazed. To sit naked in that torrent
of photons with 2B pencil and yellow pad was an
amazing bliss; I could hardly sleep nights, I was so

eager for next morning. I had already given up my daily half-aspirin, conjured into an ecstasy by January and February days of quicksilver dryness. There was no river, of course, to this commodious watering place I called the Left Bank of Tucson, only a block away from the University of Arizona, where I ambled among heavyset palm trees and through unvandalized beds of roses and pansies or, on weekends, sat on a smooth stone bench to let the well-tempered winter sun play on my face as I stared at the oranges and lemons on suburban trees only a street away on Park, Tyndall, or Euclid Avenue. Above the trees loomed the ocher, gray, or white hide of the mountains.

Each time I looked up I saw a ring of ragged peaks and thought I was living on a stage set, while, overhead, coming in so often they went almost unnoticed, jet fighter-bombers made slow-flight approaches to nearby Davis-Monthan Air Force Base, rockets in clusters under their wings, their wheels down, their turbines whining as if unfed. Not far away they touched down and then went right up again with a lunge of thunder, swarthy harbingers of the shapelessness of things to come, but in this scene as congruous as buzzards.

Friends back east were shoveling or blowing snow, while there in that mellow limbo nested at 2,400 feet among the 8,000-foot Catalinas the sun was constant, somehow generating in everyone you dealt with an exultant agitation, an almost reckless heart-

iness, you do not often find among students working
their way through college, spelling one another at the
cash registers in order to take their classes. No one
rushed. A chat was paramount. Buy your *TV Guide,*
set it down, and somebody in line would pick it up
and read it. You were free to squeeze and evaluate
their toothpaste, their mangoes, their tube of sun-
block. Early in the morning, students who lived outside of town drove up in thousands and filled lots that
created wide-open spaces among the low-set apartment houses and the rather taller dorms, which had
names like Manzanita, Gila, Yuma, and Maricopa.
Then, at about four, as the sun began to weaken, they
headed away from the watering place, and the lots
looked empty as the desert itself. Transhumance was
one word for this phenomenon, and those who
walked across walked nimbly, almost enacting that
strange sense of exemption you developed there:
snowless, iceless, rainless, in the tropic of euphoria.
It was so beautiful, so self-incising in retina and memory, that something bad was bound to happen,
though I had no idea how or when. There was almost
no weather but the sun, and it was hard not to feel
young, lucky, imperishable, born to watch the sunsets
forever as they shifted and wheeled, wan and flush,
with sometimes a horizontal spectrum above them ascending from red to violet.

A stroll down Euclid Avenue took me to The Stray
Cat, "Tucson's Party Spot," a burned-out disco-

theque whose blue-and-orange awnings had survived. The building wore them like battle ribbons and the very sight of them made me nervous, loading me with premonitions. Almost opposite stood the derelict Geronimo Hotel, chained against intruders, its ad no longer in the Yellow Pages ("Day-week-month-Phones-Elevator-Sun Deck 1 Block W of University"). Looking at that ad in an obsolete directory, I had considered moving in, but their phone was disconnected, so I knew something was wrong. What a glory once was there; the courtyard at the rear had trim little cottages overlooking mature, tilting palms, and a round cactus garden thriving and full. The place begged to be reopened by those enterprising merchants who had turned University Square into arcades of tasteful boutiques offering Indian jewelry, paintings, sculptures, and rugs, rugs, rugs, as well as shoes and books galore. For all its chic, this was an old part of town: the pastels of the walls had faded, but were subtler for being mottled; the gardens had run ripe, and the fences were squishy. There was an atmosphere, all right: for every defunct creperie a bicycle shop, for every barricaded beer parlor a temple of organic foods. It was a place of casual death and hectic rebirth, an altar of the down-and-out and the up-and-coming. It was eerie, yet a tranquilizer too.

One quiet Sunday as I strolled through the arcades to the mailbox (the post office proper was a hatch in a hallway), I came upon a student playing classical guitar because the acoustics were good and there was peace and quiet out of the afternoon sun. Passersby paused to listen and then to chat, soothing themselves, bracing themselves for the brunt of sunlight. As they walked, they studiously angled their necks and faces, connoisseurs of rays, aesthetes of tan. They used the weather as they used the neighborhood. The drugstore had no lunch counter, but sold everything from nitrateless canned chicken to plastic bags of four knives, spoons, or forks, from underwear to soup. The liquor store at Park Avenue and Sixth Street, next to the El Greco Greek restaurant, sold chocolate and ice cream. Was this the purgatorial paradise my dreams had promised me? Because so shabbily winning, was this going to be my last place? I almost wanted it to be that, abruptly shedding dreams of other idylls, such as Bermuda and Vancouver Island. I felt tuned up, yet down at heel; cheered but doomed; egged on by so much sunlight, but somehow overstimulated into a stoical passivity.

The other flank of campus, along Campbell Avenue, was duller, less whimsical, less heterogeneous. Not there would you hear a drama student on his balcony, practicing a Hamlet soliloquy for all to overhear, or smell Indian frybread being made, or see an ancient Cadillac with its windows shot out, carefully swathed in an extravagantly floral comforter. One day I saw a shooting from my window. Or rather what would have been a shooting if the husband had

not missed. Perhaps it was an operatically random
shot intended to give the impulsive Tucson police another chance to stand around for hours with paper
cups in their hands, musing on the event and keeping
cool in the near-refrigerated cold beneath an orange
or a lemon tree. The world was coming to an end
here, in magnificently lit seediness, and I could not
seem to wrench myself away from its cloning rituals,
its constant pathos.

With sunset came an almost carless quiet as the
saffron over the western range turned vermilion and
the antennas, the dishes, on top began to resemble
mutants semaphoring for help, silhouettes against an
engulfing scarlet. The lights of the high-rise towers in
the merely nominal downtown area flitted on (Tucson has no real downtown, being a centrifugal city);
but there in that dormant college quarter (a suburb
rather than a college town), something wonderful began and lasted. Globes of the softest orange light now
glowed among the palms and fruit trees like newborn
planets. A basketball court flooded with harsher light,
but there was no game, just a few players practicing
shots. A parked bus occupied half the court anyway.

The violet hour had just ended when Arab women,
a dozen at a time, came padding across the deserted
lots, all but their faces and hands wrapped in cloth,
on their way to eat, giggling and expertly changing
formation as they headed for International House. I
heard more Arabic than Spanish there. The Arabs

had come from one desert to another to study the
ecology of arid lands.

Others who crossed the lots included can collectors
who combed through the trash bins, perched the can
on its end, then accurately squashed it with a heel.
Laden with clanking plastic bags, and equipped with
a long stick having a hook at one end, these trash-
combers moved slowly, working out a life sentence,
and they had little in common with the young crew-
cut Mexican who walked boldly forth from his apartment with a cow's head and horns lashed to a
sawhorse and practiced with a lasso. Last of all came
the young, fair-haired legless veteran in his wheelchair, to which he had leashed a little terrier. On he
cruised, the dog finely adjusting its trot to the wheelchair's pace. Round the block he went, in a postmil-
itary drill, and then vanished up his ramp, into his
anonymous doorway, having survived again, his look
one of blighted eagerness. He came out when nobody
could see him, a pariah among neutrals, and must
have had his food delivered.

After him, the tang in the air became that of bar-
becues and wood smoke (it got chilly at night). Student lamps made yellow docking points. Strobe lights
on planes approaching Tucson airport flowed along
just above the roof opposite, and the electric blare of
a train—at once blustering and forlorn—reminded
me of the continent's vastness, the desert's indifference, of how, as Sartre had said, things are alone with

one another. There, maybe, because of all that limitless, much studied aridity beyond the oasis of the
city, the suburb of study turned in upon itself, in theory at least. Books opened behind picture windows,
and I wondered if those young worthies, boning up
on their thermodynamics, Tolstoy, desert sciences, or
the categorical imperative, could imagine how someone looked who sat in the sun trying to start a new
novel. Or could the youth who lassoed plastic horns,
if ever he looked up to my balcony?

Light-years from Tucson's other attractions, such
as the No-Tel Motel and the Curve Inn Motel on
Miracle Mile Strip, I found, right there at hand,
enough galleries and museums to last a year, and the
Center for Creative Photography too, whose exhibits
often changed. It was a good place to mooch around
in, entering into jubilant stagnation or just having a
long hard think. Something was looming over me, an
uninvited reef, destined to corrupt my newfound euphoria. I could feel it in the nightly chill, the whining
of those military jets: a feeling of perverse unease,
something coming in from the desert empty-handed,
to get me. I had become superstitious.

A Household God

Not in an orthodox way, but with orthodox things
bought in a store on Speedway from an anthropologist who didn't want to part with them. These were

kachinas carved by a blind Hopi Indian, a kachina or katsina being a model or doll of the full-panoplied Hopi who represents some force of nature—rattle-snake, crow, cumulus cloud, sun, early morning, spotted corn, snow, bear, cholla cactus, dew. Other kachinas personify madness, clowning, warriors, the germ god, compassion, fire, maidenhood, left-handedness, gambling, stone-eating, and silence. There are cross-legged kachinas and early-morning kachinas and bluebird-snare kachinas. Some author-ities regard them as supernatural messengers medi-ating between the harsh life of the Hopi mesas and the abundance of nature. My own version is more philosophical; I see them as iconic hymns to animism, embodiments of reverence. Carved in cottonwood root, they venerate local phenomena with teacherly zeal. I own a flute-playing doll, not truly a kachina; Kokosori, a sooty capering creature, gaudily spotted (a fire demon, I sometimes think); and a Sotuqnangu, who is the god of the heavens—thunder, lightning, the lot.

From the first, I felt that Sotuqnangu was looking out for me. Planted there on an otherwise bare table in my Tucson apartment, he faced the light and dom-inated it, and it was at him I looked when motes flicked across my vision, blurring things, making them recede and approach. Another migraine coming on, I concluded, but the attack never quite delivered itself. The eye phenomena kept on, though, about every three days; sometimes I seemed to be sucked out of my body toward whatever I was looking at; other times I felt wafted backward, horizontally levitated, as if being rudely acquainted with my surroundings. To reset my vision, I stared at Sotuqnangu's black rectangular eye slits, his triangular mouth, his upraised ax of lightning (a zigzag bolt), and soon began to talk to him about those pesky eyes of mine. Three feathers sprouted from the white cone atop his egg-shaped head. Two of them resembled X-rays of pea pods, with the peas showing buff inside, while the third fluffed forward as a forelock. How portly, solid, and omnipotent he seemed, never answering but, as the light changed around him, rotating with an almost querulous feline air. *Carved by a blind man,* I reminded myself. No wonder he mutates and, fractionally, budges about, rather like the splotches on the wall that Leonardo da Vinci made his students stare at, until the splotches moved and began to yield up all kinds of usable imagery.

I was fooling myself, of course, but someone whose eyes are acting funny has a right to horse around with a blind man's kachina. Compared to other images of that time—flight attendants playing house behind a curtain while the rest of the planeload sleeps; all those immaculate but empty cupboards that flesh out the wet bars in hotel rooms—Sotuqnangu was earthy, vivid, and tough. For reasons unknown, I knew I needed to keep him by me, he being the harbinger of trouble amid homogeneous peace. Somehow he impersonated the eerie misgivings I felt in that gorgeous place; I had been drawn to him, to his image, to the idea of him, from the first, and now I had a household god of my own, having walked him home along Speedway in hundred-degree heat one Saturday afternoon, after forking out eighty dollars. I no sooner had him than I began writing him into my latest novel, *The Place in Flowers Where Pollen Rests*, which I have always called the Hopi Novel or, if in a mood to retitle, *Where the Bee Sucks*, a title suggested to me in Paris by Marina Warner. Writing about my god, I found him invading me, beginning to accompany me on my strolls through Left Bank Tucson, on my way to class, into class, and even into lectures. He was the boss, rarely carved, and certainly never carved by anyone as by my blind man, who gave his kachinas a plump Picasso physique, a coarse final appearance as if reluctant to conceal the fibers of the wood. He was so light he might have flown, a feathered, kilted colossus with big red ears like cup handles. I learned him hard, all his details, against the days of migraine blur.

In my doleful, half-mesmerized way, I had learned from the Hopi that everything—the steam off soup, the uprooted flower—has a spirit immanent. Call it an essence, a soul, without which it cannot be itself, so you make contact with the things and creatures of the world in order to do them honor, before swigging the soup, before sticking the flower in your button-hole or mouth. A web of repercussion joins all things, which of course provides another view of my eyes than the surgical. Seeing unclearly, I merited one of those exquisite near-narratorial Hopi names, such as Sakmoisi (Chasing One Another on Green Field), Po-lípkoi'ma (Male Followed by Butterfly Maiden), and Sakhongva (Green Corn Standing). For characters in my novel I had found Silena (The Place in Flowers Where Pollen Rests), for title too, and Kuwányam-tiwa (Beautiful Badger Going over the Hill). The Hopi words were short, mostly, but the idea or vision compressed was narrative and proliferative, embody-ing, I thought, almost the same view of life as your cardiologist intends when he tells you to go to the end of the longest line to learn patience: to become a Type B instead of remaining an A. In this Hopi view of phenomena, something lyrical, antic, spry came floating back out of the eyes of ancient perceivers. After all, the Hopi is the oldest continuous civiliza-tion in North America; it knows about lasting power. From it, in crude enough fashion, I learned about do-ing everything slowly, to make it last, writing in-cluded, and about the processional view you develop if you shed the categorical thinking of an impatient civilization. Put a few Hopi words together, in iso-

lation and translated, and something of their doting
voyeurism comes through:

> loose sand around a badger hole / lightning design /
> ready to fly off nest / borrowing hot coals to build
> fire / to make beautiful surroundings / beautiful roll-
> ing green hills / life feather tied to hair / purifying
> from within oneself / magic water hoop / the west
> water that keeps rolling / object disappearing over
> flowers / before the sun has pulled down all the light /
> butterflies hatching and growing on the soil . . .

Readily identifiable phases or conditions pass into
short words, whereas such a word as *chavátangak-
wunau* (short rainbow) is an exception. The words
have been passed on, of course; and, although Hopis
do their share of intense peering, they do talk a kind
of shorthand predicated on someone's sometime
watching the behavior of butterflies or how objects
over flowers tend to vanish. So, the first in the field
of Hopi migraineurs, I might have dubbed myself
Spottily Seeing Among the To and Fro Walls, or Objects About to Disappear over Sofa. A Hopi can be
named for a process, a phenomenon of natural history, or pure botany. Read the note about the book's
compilation in Frank Waters's *The Book of the Hopi*,
paragraph five, and you will find all manner of lus-
cious names in his acknowledgments, from Wilson

Tawakwaptiwa (Sun in the Sky) to Otto Pentiwa (Painting Many Kachina Masks). We have our own versions, of course, from Solis to Smith, from Halio to Kunstler, but without, now, the long-preserved ingenuousness of the Hopi before natural phenomena and the busyness of society.

In any event, I tried to Hopi-fy my eyes, reverently attending to whatever they did instead of showing them to a physician. It was a pleasure to have these phenomena since no migraine followed them, so I took heart and got on with that novel, naked in my sunroom, engaged in a sacred dance of the imagination, hooked on atavism instead of aspirin.

My nonanalyzing mind was not yet ready to link up the things that seemed to be wrong with me and attempt a hypothesis. It did not even take into account the hives that had plagued me from childhood, sometimes weals on the insides of my arms, sometimes plateaus on my back, a quarter inch deep. For these, as a boy, I had been dosed with Parrish's Food, an iron tonic intended to remedy anemia, which I also suffered from. The hives of my manhood itched mercilessly and failed to succumb to pyribenzamine cream. Did anxiety bring them up, or something else? No dermatologist knew, and on I itched, not quite making the connection (as any Hopi would have, in a butterfly-fast suave flash) between incessant blinking and hives. A hormone mixup, maybe? No one

asked. High blood pressure? Just possibly. I adored
Tucson because it was no hallucination but, primi-
tively speaking, the most suitable place for one to
happen in, whether sacred or profane, Indian or
egghead.

A LITTLE STROKE

*I sometimes thought of a tradition observed in
European churches, which superimposed the effigy
of a dead monarch, with pomp of cloak and
majesty of chain all carved in stone, upon the poor
naked corpse lying withered and dry.*

Muscae Volitantes

At last my Arizona idyll came to an end as the temperatures went beyond one hundred Fahrenheit. Home back East, I found June a much milder matter: a mere maturing spring; leaves unrolling on the branches with parsed eagerness. I felt well enough, although having more headaches than usual and roughly the same incidence of muscae volitantes— flying flies—across my vision as in Arizona. It was the perfect place in which to resume my novel and to counterpoint that activity with household chores: the sublime versus the ridiculous.

One evening, against my better judgment as the

weather had become humid and close, I tried to fas-
ten some foam rubber buffers to the foot corners of
a bedstead, which were sharp and stuck out too far.
To do this, I crouched low, and each time I arose I
felt dizzy. The third time I got up, I felt an uncon-
trollable need to puff air as if blowing something
flimsy away from my mouth: a bunch of feathers,
maybe. Or it was to cool my lips. Something was on
the move inside me, I had no idea what, and Sotuqnangu wasn't helping out. I also felt an insensate need
to get out of that room as fast as possible, though it
was well air conditioned; my claustrophobia had
found me out and was putting me through a strict,
tormenting drill. I felt a headache coming on, but
thus far no signs of migraine or anything else. I told
myself I'd not had enough sleep and went into the
living room to watch a movie on TV. Hours later,
the visuals of the migraine began: a severe attack, all
blinding saw wheels and coruscating fortification
spectra. I was in for it again. I tried potassium chlo-
ride in water—it had seemed to work before—not
realizing it was one of the three chemicals used in
some states to cause death by lethal injection (this
was the one that made the heart, the ventricle, fibrillate and fail). After that, with the TV screen a mere
visual relic of itself as the dazzle achieved full spate,
I poured a tumbler of cognac and drank it fairly fast.
I thought I got some relief from it, although it probably did no more than blur me and start me off to

swackoland. Perspiring, I once again began to blow, puffing the feathers away from lips that felt hot and swollen. The pain got worse. I took some aspirins, then a cup of hot sweet tea, what we used to call sergeant-major tea, so strong that the spoon stood up of its own accord. The movie by now had become indecipherable, so I played some music—Bartók, I think it was—to peer at the screen by. Then I dozed off on the big round chair we called The Toadstool, little aware that my carotid or basilar arteries were under fire. No hives, but an array of symptoms was beginning to announce itself, provoked by the stuff I had taken in. Perhaps, at this point, had I had the wit and experience to head for a doctor or a hospital, a dose of something soothing might have corrected my blood pressure at least; but the migraine attack was under way, and I had drunk the cognac too. When I went to bed, I felt as if only sleep would put me right. I was going to wake with the traditional sore head, to be sure, but nothing else. The sensation of awakening with clear vision after an attack the night before was one of the most soothing and gratifying experiences I had ever known: like being reborn, like (I jump ahead to hospital analogy) a long squirt of lidocaine; like postcoital slumber, or the cool euphoria induced by beta-blockers. To be without that ghastly commotion of light turning all into a photonic circus was like rejoining the human race. You no longer felt like a Crusoe, who spent eighteen years on the island before Man Friday showed up.

My sleep was dreamless, at least as remembered, and unbroken, though of course I must have been fibrillating. I was putting a brave face on it, I suppose, aware that, as the Chinese proverb says, wasp stings a crying face. I made no link between my Tucson moments in and out of lucidity, knowing only that I had fixed the bedstead problem and nobody ever again was going to slice a shin on the sharp corners of the frame.

A Clot

I awoke rested and serene, but lazy enough to take my first cup of coffee in bed, or at least try to. My lips refused to drink, to move at all. The coffee swilled down over my chin. Within minutes my entire mouth was numb and the right side of my face paralyzed. I could not swallow, or speak clearly. I looked at my face in the mirror and saw the whole of it sagging jowly yellow, my eyes bulging and slack, my expression both tame and ghoulish.

I sat down on the couch, facing Diane, who saw uncouth and compulsive facial movements, the droop of my eyes, the sag in the skin around my cheek. She thought I was pulling a funny face, such as the characters in my novels sometimes pull, so I tried to explain, thinking I spoke clearly, trying to say "There's something wrong." She had no idea what I said, but

thought I was mumbling on purpose, limning a character or a speech mannerism I was going to work on
later in the day (novelists' houses are full of bizarre
tryouts). I tried to tell her again, and by now she had
seen the yellow of my skin as I tried to maneuver
what had gone dead. With both hands I felt at my
jaw and chin, discovering that the entire right side of
my face was paralyzed, and some of the left side too.

  She cried out and ran to me, which somehow created a pressure in the atmosphere around me; I went
to the bedroom, collected my wallet with the reso-
lution of someone determined to get at least something right, and then went to look at my face, which
had a drooped, farouche, saffron look: not the face I
expected to shave. I could walk all right, but by now
the whole of my face was numb and my left hand
and arm were beginning to feel empty, slight. Until
the ambulance came (two, actually), I sat still, wondering if I was going to see the end of this lamentable
day. What a lovely day to go wrong on, I thought; I
was supposed to call my mother in England at one-
fifteen, and clearly I wasn't going to. My mind now
occupied itself with thoughts of how to keep this
from her; it appeared to be nothing slight that I was
grappling with. I was amazed that I could still think
while being unable to speak.

  Oxygen didn't make me feel much better, but I
rather enjoyed answering the paramedics' queries in
my mauled blather, knowing they wouldn't under-

stand a word; but they did, and I knew they had seen others in my condition.

Then the return of speech in the ambulance, my schoolboy grin; the numbness of my entire left arm; the astounded male nurse who told me my blood pressure was off the map and I was fibrillating atrially. *Quel* mess, I thought; I had been going to have such a lovely Sunday. How do you feel? Chipper: just a bit incommoded. Let's go home. No, they were going to keep me. As I was wheeled into the ambulance I had flung a wave at the alarmed neighborhood—a touch of clinical bravado to show I still had a good arm to fling the ball with. I wasn't done yet. The last time the ambulance had come our way was to collect our neighbor, the Reverend Mr. Klaer, whom we never saw again. Now another wretched soul was being shifted out to the tune of a siren, and I imagined them saying to one another as I waved: Oh, he's all right, he waved, he's probably burned his hand or something. Hammering, yes: broken his thumb. Things don't happen to the likes of him. I thought that too. I had forgotten the flying flies of Tucson, the pulsing red bull's-eyes that not even Sotuqnangu could intimidate or quell.

Tanned, muscular, and really quite jovial in spite of being terrified, I lay on the narrow stretcher in the ambulance and told myself: This is out of the question. I denied all the way to the emergency room. Yet I knew I would never lecture again, never again pre-

side over a seminar, tap out a novel on the Smith-
Corona, make a phone call to my mother, or respond
to Diane when she said such things as "After many
a summer dies the *Schwann*" (this in a music store).
I was a heap of quaking paradoxes, done for so
young, and with a long novel about the Hopi to finish. I did not have Sotuqnangu with me, but my mind
threw out a loop to him, asking to be forgiven by his
sky, his lightning bolt, his tall cone of a domed head.
I was going to come back, wasn't I? Not quite perky,
I still had the milk of human defiance within me, and
my brain was working a treat. They could turn the
ambulance around now, I had recovered; it was only
a Sunday-morning triviality. Wallace Stevens would
understand. I wanted my breakfast, please. *Hell, he
wants breakfast,* I imagined them saying. *He's a game
one, this.* I won't even say goodbye, I heard myself
saying; I'm better at hello.

In fact I was having a transient ischemic attack
(said fast as TIA), or a mild stroke—although the
TIA of the textbook tends to be one-sided only. A
clot, whipped up inside my heart during fibrillation
(when the heart beats chaotically), had blocked part
of the blood supply to my brain. My pulse was 200
or so, my blood pressure 200 over 150, and all three
had no doubt been even higher to begin with. In the
ambulance I talked for the sheer joy of speech regained, but my left hand and arm were paralyzed.
The clot was on the move. My heart's atria have con-

tinued to fibrillate ever since, and they always will,
spurred on by an electrical malfunction in the sinus
node, where one's pulse begins. I had probably been
fibrillating undiagnosed for twenty years, although I
had had routine checkups. I had never been caught
fibbing, as I have learned to say, and I found that
strange; surely, if ever a heart was going to act up, it
would do so before and during a test. But the heart
has its reasons, and the mind rarely knows them.

What got me into all this? A complete answer never
comes, but I think I know the last cause in the indecipherable chain. That I should have stayed on aspirin went without saying, though I said it a thousand
times. I would have stayed uncoagulated. There was
also talk of rheumatic fever misdiagnosed as pneumonia when I was a teenager. My parents had heart
problems although living to consummate ages, my father seventy-five, my mother ninety-four. Since I gave
up alcohol, my brain is clearer, my mood sweeter,
my stomach intermittently flatter. I have learned from
children who laughingly correct the funny feeling of
their own atrial fibrillations by standing on their head
or splashing cold water on their wrist or neck. I
learned from a country doctor in a university town
how to "bear down" and so make the vagus nerve
behave. Sometimes, he told me, a loud cough would
have the same effect, the sort of cough you might
make in a public library to mask the sound of ripping

out a useful page (Jack Nicholson in *Chinatown*). I regard my heart as a host regards an alien visitor trapped in his chest, but also as an irritable friend, a lyrical incubus, who has to be humored. Or else.

Transii

I had always had a sense of being intimately linked with the stuff that I was not, if indeed I knew where I began and stuff left off. Possessed of an almost eerie sense of how different I was from earthworm, tree, and star, all of them imposingly opaque, I had an even eerier sense of overlap with them, not so much from reading as from primitive hunch. From my first chemistry set, I knew that I was an experiment too. I walked and breathed immersed in a world not mine, not made of *me*. With seemingly detached mind, I used a brain whose stuff was generally available. Something streamed through us all, and through other things, that was never itself, which is to say it had identities by proxy. It was permanent, and we were expendable.

In intensive care, whose philosophical overtone won me over at once, I who had never known a night in hospital found myself not merely a part of all I had ever seen and known, as before; I was newly connected to it by wires, oscilloscopes, tubing, and big drafts of chemicals whose nature I would eventually ponder and marvel at, like the medium contemplating his or her own ectoplasm. Dispossessed is what I felt: dispossessed of even that cozy old intimacy with nature. It had been a luxury, a mental game, and now it was being played out, proven, on my pulses, taken outside me and blown up big on screens and charts. I felt as if my marrow was being sucked away and had only been on loan. Nothing belonged to me that could not be abruptly revoked here in this functional room with only a curtain for a door: things, they, you, came in and out at speed. The transits were fast and unimpeded. The world outside the doorway, beyond the curtain, looked "down there." I lay in a horizontal shaft that not far away bent at a right angle to dispose of me.

I hung on, not a cut worm or a star starting to run out of energy, but a something somehow without a destiny. The atoms that owned me had come into their own, loud in the squeak and ping of the big EKG machine close to my bed. I had ignored the fibers in the sinus node of my heart, and now they were thrashing in chaos. I had never known catecholamines could surge and boost my blood pressure to an almost lethal level, though I had often wondered about the long headaches I got and the sense, sometimes, that my brain was being gently poached. Now those catecholamines had done their massive, silent roar through me, and I was weaker for their dominance. I was what things within me happened to. I was a guest in the throne room of juices and sludges, and it was here that heparin, a substance my own stomach made, was fed into me nonstop through an IV needle. It was here that British propranolol (*nom de guerre:* Inderal) blocked my adrenaline from reaching my sympathetic nervous system. It was here that, in need, the speeding ventricle calmed down after a long squirt of lidocaine. It was a place in which you had only a backstage identity and became just the patient: the one who suffers, your first and last names all of a sudden become Atrial Fib. Fib sounded like a lie, but the straight truth was all around you as the EKG clamored when you made the slightest move and an abortive attempt to move your bowels set all the bells ringing at once, from the bearing down (otherwise an old friend).

In intensive care, the place in which, with whatever energy I could muster, I tried to take an interest in what had happened to me: the pupil of my own mishap, asking the nurse to write out, for me to learn by heart, what propranolol is made of, and heparin, and Coumadin, and quinidine, those prompters of my latter life. Lying there with nothing to do except to dream of survival, I sometimes thought of a tradition observed in European churches, which superimposed the effigy of a dead monarch, with pomp of cloak and majesty of chain all carved in stone, upon the poor naked corpse lying withered and dry. They called this *transii,* meaning he has gone over, he has gone beyond. Where I was, the two remained fused, for a while at least, and then, if you were unlucky (never mind how hard and piously you had been trying), they floated free of each other to remain apart forever, as you "went over."

On the brink of nothing I began to think of myself in the third person: Now the use is going from his left arm again, and there is a runaway train in his chest. I became my own football commentator. But I was too blurred even to maintain the consistency of that primal decorum. Hooked up by chest and wrist, I waited for the bed to slide away down that final chute beyond the curtain. Where was the pain anyway? The pain was in a recognition that I was lucky to be there, a thing thinking about the thing I was but might not be for long. It was like being shoved back into the prehistory of humankind, waiting for my cells to move me up a rung. Impossible? Of course not; but if that was possible, then so were other preposterous things, epitomized by an Hispanic expression of sheer rage: one of the word-sets that came pell-melling into my helpless mind as I lay there. I shit, it went, into the shadow of your shave. How to go about it was the problem.

I was safe, but I was only faintly ticking over, stalled between idle and stop, in a tiny way craving something to read. I remember wanting Samuel Beckett's *Malone Dies*, for its outlandish appropriateness and homemade stoicism. I got it. I hovered. Sometimes I seemed to be levitating, whisked upward (or

winched) while gravity tugged the other way with silent skill. At other times I seemed all of me to be one
wince, one shrug, as if my body had heard something
appallingly sour and wanted to enact its scorn. The
counterpoint to this sense of invasion or dispposses-
sion was not medical; or rather it was, yet not done
by doctors. There, by my bed each day, was Diane
Ackerman, telling me, in a magnificent hyperbole of
her poet's imagination, that I was a resting lion, a
sleeping lion, like America before Pearl Harbor. I was
a lion, she insisted, and she brought me stuffed lions
to play with and befriend, big pictures of lions to gaze
at, and I half fancied I was Hemingway's old Santi-
ago dreaming of them—in my case, as animations of
an almost defunct body: picturesque babble from a
ghost that had given up. In full view of the nurses,
my lioness and I curled up on the narrow bed, she
persuading me that I could still get somewhere from
there, if only I would try. Feedback had not worked
against the paralysis of my left arm, but I think it
worked against the mental slough my body had lured
me into. Somewhere in the back of my mind an equa-
tion failed to take shape, but I had heard it, or something like it: three weeks flat on your back equals
three years of aging. I couldn't recall it, but its phan-
tom scared me back to my feet, off which I fell. Dizzy,
blacking or graying out, I clutched at my lioness and
the wall, ever on the point of knocking the IV out of
my arm. A week later, still dizzy, I was walking the

stairs within the wing while nurses monitored my heart by telemetry. I had survived to faint another day. I had learned, in irrevocable terms, that a mind stretched to a new idea never returns to its original dimensions. Was that why, only a few months later, there began the most sustained period of creativity (and reward) I had ever known? In my livelier moments in hospital I had dreamed of, and listed, the books I would write if I got the chance. Well, the chance came and, off all stimulants (decaffeinated coffee included), with a heart for once beating sometimes properly, and propranolol to give me Technicolor dreams as well as fend off migraine attacks, my brain worked better than before, I thought. No longer maltreated, it reformed and served me well.

E L I X I R S

*I have become a body-watcher, a devout
auscultator, to whom every squeeze of peristalsis
becomes a miracle of what Coleridge called is-ness,
and every irregular beat ("an irregular irregularity,"
my cardiologist says) seems an heroic elegy
evocative of the mood Stevie Smith pinned down so
well: waving while drowning.*

Testing, Testing

And so I met Dr. Dilaudid, there on duty that morning, who just had me watched and watched and watched, and only on the third day prescribed half a baby aspirin. My face came back to normal, more or less, but my arm was useless in spite of massage, hot compresses, and right-handed efforts by its owner (or brief tenant) to make it be itself again. At once there was much talk about electrical cardioversion and how important it was to get me back into sinus rhythm. Cardioversion sounded crude, whether it shocked me back into sinus rhythm or not. What if cardioversion worked, I asked, but I then went back into fib? They didn't like me to call it fib; I was being too familiar with their arcana. Well, this particular arcanum, I said, could surely provoke a stroke in somebody who had a blood clot cruising about within him. It could, and some had died from it. As it happened, I went back into sinus rhythm on my own, at once feeling serene and cool; but even as Dr. Dilaudid told me about the shift, I went back into fib, and in and out, in and out, all day long. *Homo fluctuans,* I told myself. They'll never let you out of here until the rhythm's right.

A neurologist came and tested me for sound, asking what certain noises sounded like. My facetious, inventive answers pleased him little, I could tell, even though, had I been the doctor, I would have been glad to notice the patient was capable of high spirits, was willing to fight back with what he had. It was his professional solemnity that I upset, and it did not occur to him that, if there was any solemnity to what was going on, it was mine. All this was about me, not about him or his reputation. To him, I was just an item in the long chain of cases, rather like an author to a literature student reading a survey volume. Later on, I ran into another neurologist, who flinched when I said "fib," and seemed antagonistic to the presence of the patient—like the budding cardiologist in Saint Louis, who, when I asked him if he really meant something snide about another doctor's judgment, bridled and asked, "Is this an intelligence test or what?" I, who had had little enough to do with doctors, now began to discover their nature. Some were fine, some were not; what both groups had in common was an almost total ignorance of the fact that a sick patient was not someone to spar and argue with. It was weird to be told, on the one hand, what was wrong with me and, on the other, to be spoken to as if I had all my resources going full blast to defend myself with. One anorexic cardiologist glared at me and said, "I do not like to deal with obese patients." What I, as a wordsmith, especially resented was the way some of these recently graduated sawboneses said about my incapacity to describe my symptoms. They made me angry and, in so doing, got for themselves a hyperarticulate account of their own grossness. My version of my symptoms was not simple enough for them to understand, couched in words well within their spectrum of anticipation. When the patient's blood pressure is already high, and he is predisposed to fib or is already fibbing, the last thing he should have on his hands is a personality conflict with a so-called healer. The worst example I experienced was Dr. Dilaudid, whom I one day told I had been in touch with Dr. Anis Obeid, the distinguished Syracuse cardiologist, whose name had come to me from another specialist, this one recommended by an astronomer friend. He hit the roof. I guessed he'd never heard the customer is always right. In the end he went away mollified, told that, never mind how many admirals came on board, he was still captain of the ship. I had seen this kind of arrogance before, in the military and in academe, two professions in which the rewards are not that great. It would be quite different if doctors never died and, when we dealt with them, we were dealing with a consummate superspecies whose mystery was one they utterly understood. But doctors do die, which Obeid—whose view of death is less hostile than mine—thinks a good thing because it is good for them to be parted from all that money. Pelf, I used to call it. There is no need to go into the usual complaints about the hurried look at your file as you enter. What is important to keep in focus is the concealed, dissimulated, or even ablated humanity of the doctor concerned. He or she may not wish to become too involved or identified with patients, but there is no way of dropping out of the species, or the universe, and doctors should get rid of that high-and-mighty manner, of panjandrum hubris. It can usually be found without too much trouble in any medical establishment, and it often means that the medical student in question went uneducated in the humanities and came forth as a technician, as cold with people as some academic literary theorists are with texts.

Nowadays, with M.D.'s centralized like the hubs that airlines send you to from "feeder" airports in the boondocks, doctors are increasingly on their own turf; the house call, that sometimes destructive descent into the tainted maelstrom of the plebs, happens rarely, and it is as if professors never taught (some do not), pilots flew only simulators, and banks did not hand out money. Even though it is true that doctors cannot possibly cart their best equipment with them, they should realize that patients—those who suffer—come from a different dimension, where in vainglorious optimism they hope to prosper without medical aid. When they come in for scrutiny and treatment, they are under stress; their blood pressure is already up and their hearts are beating hard. What they want next is not a confrontation, a duel. I would hate to prolong the already long training that prospective doctors have to undergo, but it might help them if they had to earn a bachelor's degree in the *human*ities first, paid for by the state. I am crying for the moon, no doubt, and I am not misconstruing those medical graduates who go on to earn a Ph.D. (the humanities are no part of their highly specialized concern). I just think of excellent doctors I have encountered, and then of those in the same profession who just don't seem to be aware they are dealing with sentient, intimidated strangers.

Not long ago, I had an abscess lanced, which was bad enough; then I had to undergo two weeks of having the wound pulled open, scraped, and drenched with hydrogen peroxide. Each time, my blood pressure climbed and my heart began to fibrillate. It took some arguing to persuade the doctor in charge that it was better not to aggravate my chronic symptoms; he had not seen beyond the abscess, and never would have if I hadn't broached the matter. Why do doctors think pain is good for people? Is it a hangover from Puritan days, if they are indeed over? Or do doctors, in a position of power, regard the rest of the race as a bunch of whiners? We are all familiar with the professional euphemisms of "you'll feel a little push" and "some pressure," after which pain electrifies your skull; but it can't be pain because the expert said only "push" and "pressure." Elements of secret society here mingle with an Inca-like disdain for the masses. Habitude has engendered hebetude, and familiarity overfamiliarity. Doctors, we drum into our skulls, are here not merely to aid us, but to solve the infinite crossword puzzle of the universe, and that holy grail is much more interesting to them than Joe Soap's pain. We have learned from Beckett, however, that one of the least admirable human traits is that we hate the sufferer because we hate pain. So, when your M.D. lets you languish and writhe, it is because he/she hates the pain you feel, therefore hates you, and won't put you out of your misery. In the long run you encounter absolutes, an absolute being something that requires nothing. Only murderers, Genet said, should judge murderers. By the same token, only those in agony should dispense painkillers. Are our doctors in agony on our behalf? Of course not; they suffer vicariously, subject, I think, to that most

dangerous of delusions: they know better than we
how we feel because, after all, they are experts and
have seen much more of this than we have. I have
heard this from so many patients that I weary of it
—when you enter a hospital, you are disrupting an
arcane, elitist system of research, whose aim, no
doubt, is to deal with diseases without the personal-
ities to which they have become attached. A severe
view, but one you come to after battling with the egos
and Procrustean assumptions of the average hospital.

The trouble with medicine is that it sees itself as a
religion. Nonmedical people believe in it too. Now,
nothing thrives on pain better than religion, which
often teaches us that what matters least of all is
the average human life—its comfort and happiness.
Medicine, like religion, is a court of miracles, but disease, unlike faith, is not a man-made thing. So you
have a court of miracles whose stock-in-trade comes
entirely from the ingenuity of matter, which is the
same wherever we go. A double whammy, this, since
you have hauteur coupled with indisputable data,
high caste with dreadful givens. Is this why the medical profession is so uppity, because its stuff is cosmic
and those diseases—Vincent's infection, vibrio
comma, telangiectasia—have not been trumped up in
Rome, Tokyo, or Mecca, even though they sound as
if first thought of in ancient Rome, ancient Athens?
There is a cabalistic, exclusive, side to medicine that
we, the suffering public, should heed; it afflicts drug

manufacturers too, who, much as the medical profession converts illness into magic, convert it into
money. It is a *profession,* as teaching is not, as law
is, and as the military and the clergy were. And a
profession has to do with power, permanence, and
secrecy. Whenever you deal with your doctor, you are
dealing with someone who deals in death and may
be conversant with yours: a special relationship to be
sure, like that with your military commander or your
clergyman (even if he counts no longer as a professional). So we have to reckon with a specialized self-
importance at the same time as an habituated attitude
to what used to be called Last Things.

Do doctors, then, feel pain belongs to God, nature,
the firmament, chemistry, or whatever? They have
not quite made the dead walk, but one day they no
doubt will, a feat that literature, music, and accoun-
tancy, bitterly emulating theology, have not been
equal to. Respect for pain seems purism of a kind:
not sadism, not power play, but some weird hankering for the phenomenon unalloyed. In other words,
the patient in pain is someone less to be made comfortable than to be harvested for data. Or pain, to
some, is parallel only, not of immediate concern, but
exactly what you might expect of nerves, and the
same with everybody. Pain is often enough of no interest, like steam rising or vapor. I keep meeting people whose pain has gone untreated, or whose loved

ones have had their pain untreated, which is to say unrecognized, unaccepted, unfelt. And I tell myself: doctors are not lighthouse keepers, symbolists, or bounty hunters. They should know and do better, perhaps indeed, if they have to choose, sacrificing a bit of knowledge to making someone feel comfortable. Are doctors when they treat us *in loco parentis* to some extent, and are we not their children—foundlings anyway?

I worry about these matters, as there appears nowadays a tremendous lack of trust in doctors, in their goodwill, their motives, their reliability, their respect for what the patient feels about his or her own life. Abstractly to keep someone alive who is merely vegetating, or to refuse assistance to a would-be suicide, argues a special interest that derives from what I have just been fixing upon in the mores of the profession —as if to say their decision over us is more sacred and imposing than our own. Their point seems to be that they consider themselves as having taken an oath that we have not. Would we ourselves behave differently if we too had taken an Hippocratic oath? In the long run we would consider common sense, ranking low our possible status as a specimen, or as an integer in some transcendental rationalization of life's holiness in the twentieth century, whose carnage has been massive. The whole issue of the living will—when we attempt to wrest control of our own lives away from those who claim to know better than we do—bears on this contest between savants and the holiness of the heart's affections.

A Very American Faith

I still have to sleep a lot, in some vague hope of nerve regeneration; the rat-poison anticoagulant I have to take for life keeps my eyes bloodshot or pink; and Quinaglute—time-lapse quinidine—kept my arrhythmias to a minimum as well as performing as a superlaxative. I cannot pretend I am unscathed. Nor, oddly enough, in some moods, do I wish to be. In other moods, I want to start afresh. I have turned into a body-watcher, a devout auscultator, to whom every squeeze of peristalsis becomes a miracle of what Coleridge called is-ness, and every irregular beat seems an heroic elegy evocative of the mood Stevie Smith pinned down so well: waving while drowning. On the not-so-good days, when my unpushed blood pools away from my body's surface and I feel intolerably hot, I try homemade maneuvers on the vagus nerve, more or less thrilled to have even this little say in my own destiny. Or I cough while holding my breath. When such measures fail, I try to accept a sweat soak as my portion and fill my mind with images of icebergs and the accursed cold pools with which cheap hotels trick out the landscape of the winter south.

I will probably never learn the full extent of what I have been through, or went through long before I had any idea that anything was wrong. Four years after my TIA, my cardiologist informed me that recurrences usually come in the first few months: something I am glad he kept to himself. "Benign cardiomyopathy," he writes on my appointment slips, warning me it isn't that benign. My life has been shortened, he says, and the heart will one day slip into a fibrillation that, far from being fatal, will become a constant; in other words, for what it is worth, and it is worth a paradise, my habitual alternation of lovely sinus rhythm and chaotic arrhythmias will go downhill into being only the latter, and I will not feel quite so good so often. I am going to sweat even more, and, under TV lamps or amid central heating turned up too high, not to mention summer and fevers, I am going to feel I am gradually being cooked. Meanwhile, I reason, the Samarkand of drugs gets bigger and cleverer; I might cheat the odds yet. Already they can cheat cholesterol with gemfibrozil, so surely the ideal anti-arrhythmic is only just around the corner, mercifully apart from the two not long ago hailed as wonder drugs and soon after removed from sale as sometimes lethal.

This is a very American faith I have in progress and remedy, tacked on to a medieval sense I have that a symmetry oversees us and provides a corrective for each and every ill. Or is it Platonic? I find myself

believing in the omnicompetence of a random universe whose apparent care for us is nothing of the
kind but only a humanized version of copious Crea-
tion. I find it harder to believe that willy-nilly the
universe does not provide than that it does. We
simply have to make our society last long enough for
the universal pharmacopoeia, with a human assist, to
heal us. I am reminded of certain dinner-table con-
versations during which one diner tells a story that
one of the other diners knows: Flaherty and Marx.
At some point in Flaherty's tale, Marx turns aside
and gives the other listeners a look of quasi-
proprietorial pride, of vicarious vindication. So too,
do we, perhaps, with a universe we sometimes find
absurd, but which is absurd only to us, rather suc-
cessfully perpetuating itself.

Or, to put it another way, the British team that
synthesized propranolol is the human tenor to the ve-
hicle of heparin, which, to be found in coltsfoot
growing in any meadow, makes the stomachs of the
cows who eat it bleed. That kind of erratic, but ultimately providential, symbiosis of invention and serendipity. Scientists head for the Amazon jungle to
capture specimens of leaves that may not exist in ten
years' time, thanks to the destruction of the rain for-
ests. Can we assume that these scientists are saving
what is going to heal us? Apparently so. Cornell University biologist Thomas Eisner says that "a large
fraction of our medicinal chemicals come directly

from nature, or are synthesized after models found in nature, or modified from models in nature." He instances the Madagascar periwinkle, which produces alkaloids used to treat leukemias and Hodgkin's disease. Because, recently, we have studied microorganisms intensively, "there has been a terrific impact on medicines—all the antibiotics, cyclosporins, ivermectin (to combat river blindness and various diseases in animals, such as worms), very recent discoveries such as taxol, from the Pacific yew, which is an anti-ovarian cancer agent, and biostatin, discovered in an ocean invertebrate. And so on."

There is chemical value in species, he contends, but if you kill them off you are closing a hidden option forever. One day, we will evolve new techniques that would have been ideal for discovering things we allowed to become extinct. The compounds in nature that *have* been found, he says, could never have been predicted, or designed by chemists and computer modelers. We never know enough about the nature of compounds, or about the chemical basis of disease. What we do, or should, know is that nothing in nature is replaceable or redundant. We should husband nature as a whole, scotching nothing, and entrusting to serendipity the role of prospector, hoping where we cannot prove. So my view of nature isn't as naive as I once thought: that slow and quiet apocalypse in which we farm nature's pharmacopoeia is a gold rush of the sublimest, most pragmatic kind. Hovering in a

dilemma, we have only prudence open to us: guard
the treasure trove at all costs; the search for the treasure isn't the treasure, not exactly, but it beats mindless tree felling hands down.

This is why such a book as *The Cornell Book of
Herbs and Edible Flowers*, a lavish compendium by
Jeanne Mackin, alerts me to a pun: the farm in pharmacopoeia. With elegant care, Mackin reminds us
how much of the external world we can ingest, sometimes for pleasure on the palate (daylily blooms
stuffed with soft cheese for an appetizer, thyme added
for piquancy to butter, jelly, vinegar, and honey), often for medicinal purposes. The ancients, for instance, used tansy to deworm children. Sweet basil
has antispasmodic and antibacterial qualities. Early
herbals recommend Roman Chamomile for headache, liver problems, and gallstones. Rue tea is good
for dizziness and female disorders. Parsley tea is good
for asthma. Lovage seeds when chewed relieve flat-
ulence. Lemon balm tea relieves coughs and may dispel melancholy. On it goes, this grateful, celebratory
record, reminding us that the world of pills and herbs
is really one and that the so-called alternative medicines touted in mass-advertised books are really the
old medicines, the sources of many brand-named
modern drugs. I remember first being instructed in
the whys and wherefores of dramatic irony, the gist
being that the audience knows something the actors
don't. Our own dramatic irony is that, as actors on

the medical stage, we every now and then recognize our affinity with some plant or shrub we had always seen as mere background. We are surrounded, as Mackin's book makes clear, by a serendipitous plenty that came boiling out of the same big bang as we ourselves and the stars. The same physics and chemistry flow through all that is, so we should not be too surprised by the shock of recognition—we open Mackin's herbarium at random and discover that hyssop, Hebrew *ezob* for holy herb, was used to cleanse temples and lepers, and is still used to flavor Chartreuse. A poultice made from its leaves may be useful in treating insect bites. How gratifying, and perhaps not amazing, to be so intimately tied to nature, the only chore remaining being the identifying and exploring of as many plants as possible. The increasing number of such books as these demands what the politicians used to call an agonizing reappraisal—of our vegetation. Instead of living in a hostile element that smothers and surfeits us, we have slept between the pages of a colossal herbarium so far only skimmed. The example of foxglove—source of digitalis since the eighteenth century—instructs us, and William Withering's classic, *An Account of the Foxglove, and Some of Its Medical Uses* (1785), instructs us even more (the lethal dose may be only three times the effective one).

Go-getters as we may be, in a tradition reaching from Francis Bacon, who saw the reasoning scientist

of the Renaissance as a *buccinator novi temporis*
(trumpeter of the new era), we are going to fare better
with something like the wise passivity recommended
by William Wordsworth, to whom daffodils were
holy, enacting a theodicy—at most a speaking forth
of God, at least a nature (or Nature) better equipped
than it had any need to be, with undreamed-of compounds lurking in wait to combat undreamed-of diseases. I guess that is my own version of "Gaffer"
Wordsworth, on whose poetry I was brought up,
from ten onward—a country boy reared on all manner of peasant superstitions, the most recent of which
goes something like this: Here at the level of a botany
whose ancestry came from the stars, I have something
wrong with me that an Amazonian leaf, born so far
to blush unseen (or undeciphered), may put paid to.
Call it a star ricochet, a tangent of usefulness coming
at random into being amid the intermittent fidget that
evolution is. Who can resist such copious magic?
Who dare banish it to the sidelines in the interests of
lumber or cleared ground?

The beloved chemistry set of my boyhood has
come back to me, with its litmus papers, its tubes of
potassium sulfate and calcium carbonate, its Bunsen
burner and tinful of rattling strontium nitrate; but, in
order to play with this new version of it, I have to
put my carcass on the line and rejoice at its being
there. I do. Each day is a pageant, an experiment, a
ravishing communion with wumphing, impersonal

stars. Death, as one of my students wrote, intending
something quite different, is a plague for which there
is no known anecdote. Perhaps. All I know is that
not to have told the anecdote or story of it all, to
oneself or to others, would make me feel less powerful than having told. We live in a precarious plenty
lent us.

A Ghost

When I looked up from my writing pad to the
chasm of sunlight in the rough direction of the Tucson basketball court, I saw the child in the man, but
never what came to me soon after I came out of hospital and, stoked up on Inderal, began dreaming
dreams of caustic precision. The dream that upset me
most was the one in which my seventeen-year-old
self, at about the age I went to university, or came
back from sitting Oxbridge scholarship exams and
returned with all my stuff in a cardboard box tied
with the cord from my bathrobe, confronted me with
fierce disappointment and asked me: What have you
done with your life? Couldn't you have done better
than this? You have let me down, you feckless elder.
He was an articulate son-of-a-bitch, all right, and in
the dream I merely gibbered in return. There he was,
worn out, rings under his eyes, his hands trembling
with rage, fresh from the high assault of the examination papers, not having slept for a week, and there

I was, a crock, a wreck, a physical flop who, having failed to take care of himself, had jeopardized his future, his gifts, his very heart. Where, inquired my junior inquisitor, is the physical prowess you once had? You were a superb athlete, a high-class jock.

If only he would go away, I thought, whether sent by Sotuqnangu or not; the one thing he must learn is never to upset the patient. Keep his blood pressure down.

He never showed up again, but I have not recovered from that teenaged assault within the bowels of memory, and I wonder what else lurks therein, to chide and shock. Perhaps for as long as I obey Obeid, he will remain in abeyance, a wound always closing but never healed. To be like him, to be him again, I lack the inexperience. His heart was broken by his hero, and he does not forgive.

While I was still in hospital, and long after I left, a seminar met weekly to figure out what was wrong with me: neurology or cardiology? Perhaps the trouble lay in the basilar artery? Perhaps lifelong migraines were the root of all my ills? The debate went on, as unresolved now as then, but at least abandoned. Yet the worry lingered in my head. Why did that anemic, hive-afflicted boy who blinked nonstop become the patient he became? Again and again, I the medical voyeur, like the person with a toothache jabbing tongue into the agonizing cavity, thought back to the night before my stroke and scoured its every cleft, fondled its fiber, wondering not only what had caused it, but what it had really been like. What had this experience been, in which I had appeared to recede from the human species? One summer evening, much later, I had strolled home and seen, en route, in the gloom, a student crouching to feed a squirrel, in his mouth a lit cigarette. Even as the tame squirrel perched erect, hands up, to receive some tidbit, the young man released a cloud of smoke, and its aroma as it dispersed in the lazing air was fecal, as if his innards were close behind the smoke, drawn upward and outward by it, floating toward me with some taint of death. The smell was brackish, ammoniac, tobacco-sweet, and I quickened my step away from him, I the nonsmoker in the valley of the shadow.

ON BECOMING BIONIC

At first I thought he had arrived with a bola, the rope used in Argentina to entangle a steer's legs as the weighted ends coil around them. Then it seemed an anchor, a yo-yo, a silver disk on a string. Very much a toy.

The Imminence of Dr. Frankenstein

Seven months after the TIA, my heart began to slow down to thirty beats per minute; for some periods it was inert for as long as seven seconds, and it would soon be inert for longer. I had been to see Dr. Obeid in Syracuse and had stayed there overnight so as to wear a heart-monitoring device called a Holter for the required twenty-four hours. I was back home, cooking a meal of Chinese vegetables, when the phone rang. "I want you here in hospital tonight," Obeid said, unusually imperious for him. "I feel fine," I told him. "We're just going to have Szechuan West. I'm cooking it right now." He told me to enjoy the

fruits of my own cooking and then get my replenished
or affronted body through the sleet and fog to hospital, where a bed awaited me. He that's coming shall
be provided for, I heard. What a cozy threat. "You're
in trouble," he said. I demurred. He spoke with Diane
then, convinced her, and we were there by ten
o'clock. I had so much wanted to think I was through
with medical procedures. The one thing that cheered
me was Obeid's standing order to all hospital staff to
let me sleep in, until at least 8 A.M. Unheard of, this
fiat brought patients and doctors alike from all over
the hospital just to gawp at the enormous placard
outside my door. Obeid believed in the usefulness of
sleep, like Shakespeare, but in pacemakers too: I
needed one, he said, as soon as possible. It was the
only thing to do. "Remember?" he said. "I told you
it would come to this. It has. You'll be better than
ever." I felt chagrined that Inderal, Coumadin, and
Quinaglute hadn't been enough; now we were going
to the cutting edge of technology for a contraption
as complex as a World War II bombsight. Oh no,
much cleverer: Saint Francis, one of Obeid's idols,
would no doubt have approved, so long as I accepted
the implant humbly.

I had various questions for the surgeon, Dr. Pradhan, when he arrived, and he breezed through the
answers, telling how many pacemakers he had implanted, in what kinds of patients, and where he had
trained in India and the United States, and with

whom. He jibbed, though, when I asked if he would recommend this procedure for a member of his own family. Right now, he said, there was no case to consider; he could not deal with such a question in the abstract. The empiricist had met the novelist and worsted him. But he certainly dealt with another question I posed: "Are there times when it is utterly imperative to implant a pacemaker? Are there times when someone does the thing a bit too soon?" Yes, yes. But there was nothing premature about this, he said. He spoke of heart block, a phrase that had not come up before, although, shopping around in the *Physicians' Desk Reference* and the *Physicians' Drug Manual,* not forgetting the *Merck Manual,* I had become familiar with such gems of cardiological jargon as *pulsus paradoxicus,* the footprints of Wenckebach, salvos and cannon waves. The imagery had power and stealth. Mobitz 1 and 2 suggested master plans from World War I, or prison camps from the war that followed, and bigeminal beats sounded positively musical. I had a strong emotional interest in such jargon; its esoteric poetry was what went on inside of *me.* In the superstitious way that seems peculiar to Western intellectuals from Faust on, I wanted to find out how things worked or did not work. I wanted to know the invader's taste in symbolism, his response to the chamber music of Franz Schmidt. If you have to go through all this, I told myself, you're entitled to the whys and wherefores; they give you that sense of minimal but not altogether abolished control. You feel less passive, less of a patsy. An illusion? Probably so, as I was to find out.

Then I asked about complications attending the procedure, all of course in the interests of what I called knowledge for its own sake; but I also wanted to frighten myself to death, I suppose, and then prove myself to myself in setting such terrors aside and going ahead. With expressionless candor, Dr. Pradhan, who had just been chatting about his daughter's wish to study creative writing at one of several universities, went down the list, from an air embolism when the lead is threaded into the vein to myocardial hemorrhage when it passes into the first chamber of the heart. The target tip might also migrate or be rejected. The lead might erode. I might get an infection, or muscle spasms, or hiccups. He had never had a fatality or a severe mishap, but he had colleagues who had. Nothing precluded some complications, some of the most unanticipated interactions of unknown factors. For half an hour he just explained the mainstream snags while I studied the labyrinthine intaglios of his cuff links.

"Do I really need the thing?" I asked, as if I were there for a bypass; but the realization had bitten home. A pacemaker was another alien presence, an invader once in never out. It was not just a patch applied, a decal, but an incubus. I sensed the imminence of Dr. Frankenstein, who was going to send me stumbling back out into the world as a well-wired freak at the mercy of microwave ovens and thunderstorms, insect-repelling wave-emitter boxes and airport security barriers. I was on the brink of joining a minority of some half million, doomed never again to dive into water or play body-contact sports, obliged to sit always on the left in buses, planes, and trains, with the vulnerable part of me wadded away from falling suitcases and key-loaded pockets. Already I flinched from imprudent contacts and became, in a flash, as obsessed as John Milton became with Pelops, dismembered and offered as a mince to the gods, but restored by Hermes except for the piece of shoulder already devoured by Demeter, which had to be replaced by a chunk of ivory. Maybe I would run into Pelops, and Demeter, his surgeon, in some bar for *mutilés de guerre,* in the Mutants' Lounge. Would we dare expose our broken bodies in the wading pool? Would I be as afraid of magnets as he of tusks?

One thing was certain: the probe would always be in that intimate red nest of the heart. Dr. Pradhan reiterated my cardiologist's bleak prophecy that, one day soon, I was going to collapse because my heart had paused too long. Or I was going to drop dead. That nonanswer overrode all my questions and quibbles, at least as Obeid and Pradhan saw it.

All the same, a big piece of me wanted to squirm away home and risk it. My blood pressure had re-

mained stable on its medication. My mind was working a treat. I persuaded myself that I could sense
when the wooziness was going to hit; all I had to do
was sit down fast and wait it out. I felt chilled by
Pradhan's unemotional recital of what could happen
to you in even the most expert hands, but he was
citing the odds, the body of knowledge, with I supposed the same confidence as Cambridge University,
in bold type in its pamphlet *Information for Students
from Overseas,* says: "The address of any College is
simply its name followed by Cambridge, England."
Imagine saying that in the age of postal and zip codes,
with no guarantee of delivery or return. The address
of anything may be so-and-so, but is *that* where your
letter will end up? There are always odds, to the most
trivial procedure, and I marveled even then, wrought
up as I was, at the mind's capacity to want to know
the unknowable, in Macbeth's brisk phrase, "to jump
the life to come." I grilled Dr. Pradhan good and
proper, but in truth badly and improperly, as any
self-styled analytical mind might.

Before he left, I agreed tentatively to go through
with the procedure, but he himself insisted that at any
point up to about two in the afternoon, tomorrow, I
could back out, delay, or cancel. His ego was not in
the least involved in my choice any more than it had
been in my questions, and it would not come into
play during the operation either. An appropriate card
went up above my bed, and I was told, just in case I

went ahead, presumably after an evening's intense thought, not to eat anything after midnight, which, however, I habitually do, as that is when my workday begins, usually lasting until four.

Around dinnertime, Dr. Obeid stopped by and in his gently magistral way told me to pull back, to stop trying to summon up, warts and refinements and all, a body of knowledge I had not been trained to understand. The answers to some questions were useful to me, he thought; the patient is entitled to be vigilant and self-concerned; but the answers to many other questions were so recondite, so much involved with chance, that I had best leave them alone. Theologies, I thought, give various answers as to the nature of God. They don't hesitate to supply positive answers in the absence of evidence. But theologies do not go to the operating room, not in that sense anyway. I look back with some amusement on my behavior, I the only too willing celebrant of enigmas natural or man-made hacking my way through the night and fog of luck. I remember thinking it was like being in a sailplane and not flinching back from the motion of the plane but going with it as your head pressed hard against the so-called tumble home of the canopy. Or it was like being in water, as a learner swimmer, and letting the water have you because, in having you, it buoyed you up, unlikely as that seemed. It was the surrender I was backing away from, loath as I was to commit myself to absolutes and homogeneous stands. In the end, though, I accepted what I was told, and what I knew, what I signed. Medicine is no more an exact science than it is an exact art; which is to say it is a science and an art as well, but only as exact as it can be made to be.

How my mind had buckled and flexed, asserted itself then cringed away. I had wanted it and it alone to find out for me the right thing to do, to be my surgeon and cardiologist in one, just like that. The last thing it had wanted to do was trust blindly. Now here was this top-notch humanist of a cardiologist telling me to take him and the surgeon on trust. It sounded so nineteenth century, so like the vaunted leap of faith. "We do not want you to *be* an individual," he said, "not for such a purpose as this. We want you to be average, typical. It's no use making the surgeon nervous or overcautious, feeling he has been put on his mettle and must prove himself beyond measure. The very search you subject him to may produce just the flaw you fear." I could see his point, though part of me demurred, and always would. I recalled second-to-second compounding of interest: impossible because the instant occupied by calculation made the calculation obsolete—at least if you are working with paper and pencil, a more or less stone-age compounder—and because with time, as with a crumb or with a bead of water, there is no indivisible minimum. What I wanted was as hypothetical as that, just as theoretical. All I could ever get was a list of known mishaps, but my impulse to trifle with the minutiae of chance amounted, I eventually saw, to morbid vanity. No doubt the two worthy doctors would trust my literary taste, but their lives would not depend on it (unless they took an apocalyptic view of letters), whereas, in theory at least, to trust them was to gamble just a bit with my life. All right, then, I *am* gambling, I told myself; as in 1955 when you went up in an Avro Anson with Freddie Knapper over the North Sea and then wave-hopped with him until one wing hit a wave and we lurched, lucky, away, off to seven thousand feet to cure the shakes.

I remembered a distinguished scientist upon whom the local hospital refused to operate for peritonitis because he was world-renowned, and they didn't want a scandal on their hands if things went wrong, as they just a teeny bit might. They wouldn't gamble, so why should I? Why should he, except that he wasn't in much of a condition to deliberate the rights and wrongs. In the end he went to a veterans hospital in the same town as I was in now.

Cuddling a Tiny Propeller

What shone in Dr. Pradhan's hands when he entered, shooting the white frost of his cuffs, was what I could have. At first I thought he had arrived with a bola, the rope used in Argentina to entangle a steer's

legs as the weighted ends coil around them. Then it
seemed an anchor, a yo-yo, a silver disk on a string.
Very much a toy. Then I saw he had brought two of
them. Maybe I didn't want to believe he had brought
the real thing, and I disliked the idea that something
he could implant in my very own heart, my very own
chest, he could also swing around in front of me with
an airy playful motion that revealed his mystery, let
him flaunt his wares. I also shrank from the notion
that he found his toys irresistible, knowing that all
he had to do was twirl his bauble around and I would
yearn to have him do me. If I could resist the top-
line VCR, I could resist this, couldn't I? The crypto-
Luddite in me surfaced once, then dwindled away
even as I rationalized my old-fashioned taste in
writing machines. State-of-the-art flawlessness didn't
matter when I was typing words or watching the latest Kurosawa; but for something that would make
me bionic?

I saw two pacemakers, each in convex titanium
like small cigarette cases, from each of which curled
a lead encased in pliable metal mesh with, at the tip,
a tiny version of the chimney sweep's brush: a probe
with a few flanges sloping backward at forty-five degrees. *These,* Pradhan said, would embed themselves
in the wall of the ventricle and, if I was lucky, make
themselves permanent by building up scar tissue
around them. They would snag and hold, hooking
me like a fish.

How many beats my heart skipped, or threw in extra, at the sight, I have no idea. I felt sickened. He would slide the probe through a vein, and the flanges would bend back along the lead, giving way easily as the probe passed from the vein into the right atrium, where much of my trouble was to begin with. I didn't want to be threaded thus. Then it would go through the tricuspid valve into the right ventricle, the holy of holies. I fingered the flanges, briefly a thoracic surgeon with all that power over people's rib cages, wondering if they couldn't be made even more pliable, easier to smooth back as the probe slid ahead. Wouldn't they catch on something while going in? Once inside the ventricle, they were supposed to spring outward again to snag the soft pulp inside. Round and round my mind went, repeating the abomination to exorcise it. Surely the lead would slip and then, like some zany metal butterfly, waft around, touching off twitches and convulsions wherever it landed, scraping and abrading, making me gasp. Wouldn't there, *won't there,* I asked, be a leakage when the tricuspid valve has the lead going through it? Good question, Pradhan said (he who did two of these operations each afternoon). But no: the pliable triple petals would mold themselves around it—no leak. I posed other questions. Asking questions, you feel less powerless, yet you end up not much wiser or even better informed. No, this had a lithium iodide battery, not plutonium, no longer much used, and it might last as long as ten years, depending on how much the heart demanded of it. This was a demand pacemaker, after all.

When, I wondered, would my mind stop going off at tangents, eager to escape a brutish truth? To me, the procedure seemed barbaric, although not of course to him. What bothered me was not so much the slit beneath the collarbone that would enable him to slide the shiny shape into place amid the muscles and behind the subcutaneous layer, leaving me with only a bulge whose crest was the sealed smile of the scar. At that I jibbed not much. What set my teeth on edge was that slithering lead, when it went past the defenseless portals at my core, silver interloper where the sun had never shone and where there was never rest. My heart would be cuddling a tiny propeller forever. If it came loose, could they get it out, with what I now thought of as the *barbs* going the wrong way? Surely they would catch. I fondled the flanges, forcing them forward toward the probe. Wouldn't they tear me apart if they had to come out? That each pacemaker cost five thousand dollars seemed beside the point. I was backing down again.

Then I realized that, instead of fending off all these images and tangents, I must allow them full play as my head's means of getting used to the idea; my imagination was translating for me, the barbaric into the tender, and I broke through to the palatable comparison that had been at the back of my mind all along. Instead of that chimney-brush lead, I was going to have the pink and velvet-gentle pistil of a hibiscus slid into my vein, with five red-spotted stamens in the vanguard, behind them the shank of the pistil and the tiny wire whisk of pliant golden commas that were the pollen. When the mind is foiled, it feeds itself some bizarre things. It worked, though, almost like self-hypnosis, and I felt very much outside myself, allowing them to do all this to someone else, into whose most private thoughts and sensations I could peer. If I *had* to be implanted, then it would be with something like this, alien but somehow semifriendly. If being imaginative is what scares you most, then use imagination to come to terms. I did. Once in, having graced its passage with an ocher talc, the hibiscus-pacer would merge at once with the just-as-soft mucosa at its destination, fusing heart of the flower with the heart of me. I had never before thought of metaphor as a means of anesthesia, but of course it was, and I had not been reading and writing with enough care.

At first I hesitated at almost every turn. Would the thing break loose? I must not bump into people or their stuff. Was I, like some possessors of this gadget, going to develop the so-called time-bomb complex, in which I thought it would go bang or begin to tick? I had been told that, when it was responding to demand, I would perhaps feel a twitch or a tickle, a little throbbing, and I did. A little lead soldier had

taken up residence in a soft sentry box deep inside
me, and he would sometimes march up and down,
his feet making a small battuta on my suet. If I got
worked up enough, I would be able to switch him on,
because then my heart would be fibbing, skipping and
missing, doing its old syncopated dither, sometimes
so profound and sustained that parts of my body—
my vocal cords, for instance—worked improperly
and my voice went limp, unrecoverable. To calm
him I would resort to feedback, whispering: What a
lovely, silky heart you are, how could I ever do without you? Away with what the school of Hippocrates
said about you: that you bubble like boiling vinegar
and creak like a new leather strap. It's you that's
state-of-the-art. To such blarney my heart sometimes
responded, caught off guard, at least until my mind
overheard itself and delivered the unfibrillating fib to
the fibers of the heart muscle, which knew a con man
when it heard one. And so back to cardiac chaos.

People have addressed their carcinomas, their ul-
cers, their aneurysms, so why not come up with a
few sweet phrases aimed at an incubus intended to
do some good? As if saluting Man the Machine. As
if rejoicing at having what I called a titanium tit. If I
could get my mind off it for long enough, a week,
say, and then even longer, I might learn to live with
it, instead of in spite of it. I had coaxed myself to
keep calm through the operation that implanted it,
even though during it we had had an electrical failure

and, at one hairy moment, an onset of ventricular tachycardia that made me feel I had a speeding dynamo in my chest, which was going to break loose and scatter my viscera like so many sponges. At another point, because my heart kept kicking the pacemaker lead out, they had almost decided to cut their way through the front of my chest and install the electrodes directly on my heart—a much more complex job. In the end, however, the tip of the lead bit and snagged, the ventricle failed to punch it loose and slowed down, and the front of me stayed uncut.

I walk uneasily away from microwave ovens, though, knowing as I do that only leaky ones can harm me, and I smile at the pseudo-VIP treatment meted out at airports, where I go around the magnetic sensors and get hand-scanned, braced ever for the litany that goes (often enough): "It wouldn't hurt you to go through, you know." Little do they know. They let me through, I reason, not so much because the magnetic sensors might start my pacemaker off or halt it as because I would keep their buzzers ringing forever. I would never get through to the other side, even if alive, until I had pretended to be my own hand baggage and allowed myself to be X-rayed so that they could see clearly what had been planted in my chest, below the collarbone.

Charons

After my first year of being bionic, I rather began to relish the lore of it all, always having a good chat about titanium when I left from Ithaca, New York, or University Park, Pennsylvania, sometimes referring to a much classier metal we did not yet have, called unattainium. People get to know you and your condition, and a whole gamut of discreet nods and waves ensues, though from time to time a female operative will delay you until she has mustered the pluck to hand-scan you, which operation she mistakenly thinks entails intimate frisking. You learn to laugh even while your civil rights are being violated, even at the chronically inept, who yell to a colleague down the line, "He's got a pacemaker, Frank."

"A *what?*"

"Pacemaker, I said."

"Yeah? So what? What's that?"

"Pace-maker."

"*You* do him, Al."

Any shred of embarrassment I ever felt in the beginning has long since gone. There was the woman security guard who said, "You don't mind if I feel you up some?" (She did not have a hand scanner.) "You're used to doing that," I said as I passed over from beyond the pale into Secureland. She stiffened into her tunic, looked sideways, and told me to put my hand over my pacemaker and keep it there. The

guards who knew least about this business were at
the TWA terminal, JFK; at Lambert Airport, Saint
Louis; the old terminal at Sacramento, California;
Houston, Texas; and College Station in the same
state (in College Station they make you wait until
everyone else has gone through, even if you arrived
first, thus, as I see it, abridging your civil liberties).
You appraise the gates as you approach, noting those
that have no space for you to pass through, not until
they make one by tugging aside one of the bollards
that support a plastic rope. They peer at me, these
Charons: I don't look old enough for such a prosthesis, whereas of course many children have pacemakers and wear them with aplomb. The crudest encounter I have had was at Syracuse, New York,
where the guard felt me up for weapons and other
metal, then, as I departed from his orbit, yelled, "You
want to get some of that weight off, buddy boy."
Even a vulgar fraction of a half-wit can occasionally
serve the Third Reich. The most bizarre experience I
have had with security was at Charles de Gaulle Airport, Paris, where, after I told the guard I would need
to be hand-scanned because I had a *stimulateur car-
diaque,* he waved me through everything, checking
only my hand baggage. I could have had a bomb in
my pocket. The most attentive overture to pacemaker
wearers is at the British Airways terminal at JFK; as
you approach the security gate, you discover a large
sign lettered in gold on brown (discreet), reminding

pacers (as I sometimes call them) not to go through the gateway, but to inform the operative. Ah, I thought when I first saw that sign, at last somebody knows we are in the world, mingling and almost passing muster. They have us in mind. Was there perhaps an incident? Or does the sign come about because somebody of sensibility and awareness made a fuss in some committee? It is joyous and warming thus to be thought of before your arrival. He that's coming has indeed been provided for, I remember thinking. A plus for anticipation and human *nous*. No such sign at Heathrow, however, and you wonder why the colonies are still outdoing the home office. Then you remember and wonder no longer.

I had no sooner got accustomed to the weekly or fortnightly blood test, to check my clotting time and thus the efficacy of my Coumadin dose, than I had to get used to another rigmarole, which tests the pacemaker by telephone. With an electrode on each index finger, I transmit my pulse to the master computer, where a specializing nurse monitors the test, and then pass a big blue doughnut of a magnet over my pacemaker, setting it off, and it goes *cheep-cheep*. Or it should if the battery has not failed. If it has, as one day it will, my heart-block problems will recur and I will become dizzy all over again. In other words, the pulse in the atria will not get through to the ventricles, or in not very good array. The surgeon removes the old battery and implants a new one, which is bound to be smaller. If you last long enough, I presume, you ultimately receive a battery the size of a quarter and go into your grave with one of the nimblest engines in the world frantically trying, in the very temple of your chest, to restart the arrested heart. A vestige. A spoor. A love tap. Just as if it were two paddles and not just an accelerator. You sense a chance of immortality here, turning into a Frankensteinian metronome.

Having come this far, I want to be as mechanically foolproof as I can; but in order to become that you need to have implanted in you a different kind of pacemaker, which delivers a powerful shock sufficient to halt a fibbing ventricle (the easy way to sudden death). People who have these in them go unconscious briefly and fall when the life-saving shock goes off, but they get up in good shape, ready to resume: reprieved, reprogrammed. I sometimes wonder how many contraptions I will need to have, how many I *can* have, before they start getting in one another's way. My problem is electrical, and that is perhaps why I have come to dote on Mary Shelley's famous book, on all the spin-offs from it, but most of all on the passion to bring the dead back to life that dominated the fevered imaginations colluding at the Villa Diodati in the miserable summer of 1816, when the dust from the Tambora volcano in Indonesia was flying over Europe. New Frankensteins laid their hands on me when I was on the brink of being

naught and engineered me back, not with galvanom-
eters and lightning conductors, but with little clever
motors (and those other motors we call pills). I wish
Mary Shelley, and Percy Bysshe, a pacemaker or two
to play with, and I marvel not at the eyes in Mary's
nipples (although in intensive care you believe in anything) but at the toy that tweaks me. Sometimes,
picking up the phone and connected to California
within seconds, or sending in only a slightly longer
time a fax to Paris that will slither out of their machine coiled and slimy, I pat my pacemaker and rejoice at the celerity of our toys. The instant my heart
rate slows or gives an erratic reading because I am
fibbing and therefore not giving a steady count, the
demand exacts a response from the electronics in my
chest, and I continue, far from perfect or regular, but
fudged through again, propped up by a beam of crys-
tal light that has not read Descartes but knows me
inside out. How moving, I think, as I whisper to California and prompt Paris. I tweaking them, my 8423
Spectrax tweaking me.

I know, of course, that the side effects of porting
this gadget include body rejection phenomena such
as local tissue reaction, muscle and nerve stimulation,
infections, erosion of the pulse generator lead, embolism, cardiac tamponade, and transvenous lead-
related thrombosis. Defibrillators and electric cautery
threaten me always, as do large power tools, burglar
alarms, arc welding units, resistance welders, and in-

duction furnaces. I try to be careful, even in libraries, whose checkout mechanisms are mostly no threat, but I do have a sense of moving through some electrical no-man's-land whose contraptions want to send me burly, overpowering messages apt to turn me to soot. You can't be aware of everything, though, even if you have read all the caveats in the technical manual that comes with the pulse generator. My roving, not altogether pragmatic eye alights on Figure 12: Positioning Unipolar Pulse Generator, and notes its unbiological sketch of the subcutaneous pocket into which the gadget goes. I see a hand as gloved and featureless as those hands in old-fashioned astronomy charts, pointing out a certain star, and the clean-cut edges of the gap. No blood. No mess. No surrounding anatomy. If only surgery were always this dry.

FIBBING

I fib most after I have eaten and the vagus nerve, the enormous "wandering" thing that supplies the viscera with automatic fibers, has been disturbed; don't ask me why, but eating sends it bonkers.

Sinus Rhythm

I have had enough of data: rubber grommets and hex wrench tools. I am back at my telephone and fax, pestering friends and colleagues, richly delighted to be still alive, like a whale, Coleridge's "sole unbusy thing," pointing out to someone, who cares less about such things than I, that in the movie of *Death in Venice* the young boy who appeals to Aschenbach does something with an orange that no Polish boy would do: he imparts to it, as he tosses it to and fro, what a cricketer would call leg spin, an American "English," with the hand crooked in a special way. I look up Luchino Visconti's movie in my video guide, wondering if the boy is Mark Burns, very Brit, or Björn Andresen, and now begin wondering if Dirk Bogarde taught Björn Andresen—if it was indeed he

—how to play cricket, corrupting him in ways never dreamed of by the sin-licking Thomas Mann. Such ruminations go on while a petty throb in my chest just below the collarbone gives me a decent beat, good enough to dial this miracle to California or Paris, simply, I suppose, to show to myself that I am a citizen of the wired-up world, like Monsieur Jourdain in Molière's *Le Bourgeois Gentilhomme,* speaking prose—or electronics—all his life without knowing it. Behind this minor triumph of the lower ether lies the scenario of my monthly pacemaker checks. Am I in or out of sinus rhythm? Is you is or is you ain't my baby? For a whole year I fibbed at each test, already doomed, I thought, to the final stage of deterioration, although perhaps achieving sinus rhythm during sleep. For a period of six months, however, and more recently, I was in nothing but sinus rhythm: obviously getting better, although no doubt fibbing in sleep. Maybe it is always fifty-fifty, a durable Janus of the heartbeat. I know this, though: to fib is to be hot and sweaty, with what seems a live rabbit frisking about in your chest, so much so that you almost dare not move, or speak, or breathe. There seems altogether too much busyness in there. To be in sinus rhythm, though, is to feel cool and static, no motion at all in there, no perspiration on the outside, as if the heart were winking. I look up "sinus" just to be sure and find this:

Sinoatrial node—a small mass of tissue made up of Purkinje fibers, ganglion cells, and nerve fibers, embedded in the musculature of the right auricle of higher vertebrates, representing the remains of the sinus venosus of lower forms, *serving as a pacemaker to the heart* [my italics], and transmitting the impulse to beat by way of the Purkinje's network to the auricles, the atrioventricular node and bundles, and the ventricles—called also *sinus node.*

Thus almost helpful Webster, who on the same page reminds those with double pacemakers that *sinus* probably comes from *ǵiri,* "bosom" or "lap" in Albanian, and the Serbian verb *zaošijati,* meaning "to bend." Really? *Zaošijati?* I will settle for lap or tuck, envisioning the spark in the aboriginal pouch, the spark that faded out in me or refused to travel from atrium (or auricle) to ventricle, downward, of course. How refractory can a spark get? This word "sinus" is the same sinus as turns up in the sinusoid of mathematicians, but nothing to do with anything Chinese. My own knowledge is cruder, telling me that I fib most after I have eaten and the vagus nerve, the enormous "wandering" thing that supplies the viscera with autonomic fibers, has been disturbed; don't ask me why, but eating sends it bonkers. I tend to be in sinus rhythm most often after I wake and the assorted vicissitudes of the day have not yet made their noise in my system. In the old days, in hospital, when I shifted from fib to sinus, I used to feel I was levitating. A sharp thud took place inside me, followed usually by a keen plucking sensation in the region of my heart, as if André Gide's Promethean eagle had sunk a hooked beak into some of those truly tubular Purkinje fibers and begun to tug. I told the doctors who were tending me, but they showed no interest. They should have done. One of the most dangerous moments in the fibbing patient's life comes with the shift into sinus rhythm, when the blood that has been whipped almost to a cream by the fibrillating atria (or auricles) can get an emissary in the form of a clot out into the bloodstream, and with the big heft of sinus rhythm behind it, shoving it, speeding it, to where it might lodge. When you come back to normal, you are in peril, even as that gorgeous feeling returns of being sedate and cool—much like the eerie peace conferred by propranolol. Of course, if you go from fib to sinus while on Inderal, you feel twice as well, but, unless you're anticoagulated and can't clot, you're in the immediate running for a thrombosis and some kind of stroke. I have rehearsed this threat thousands of times, always ending with thanks to Coumadin, whose other name, warfarin, comes from [University of] Wisconsin Alumni Research Foundation . . . I have forgotten the rest, but it could be And Research Initiation Network. Sometimes, in a perverse mood, I pick up a carton of d-Con and read the list of constituents, and there it is, the chemical that makes rodents bleed to death, the same one as brings me occasional bouts of red-eye that take a couple of weeks to fade. I have found, during seminars, that a point made with an eye like Mars to back it up has actual chances of survival. Usually, when I awaken and see that carmine blotch I know my blood pressure has gone up during the night and my thinned-out blood has seeped. Already flagged with a Post-it, the appropriate page in my *Merck* announces that such a hemorrhage might be subconjunctival, vitreous, or retinal. The first, which it always is, the book calls a "gross extravasation of blood beneath the conjunctiva." Reassurance is adequate therapy, and nothing else works. You have to be prepared to look weird for half a month. Coumadin, which Obeid admiringly thinks a nasty drug, can turn your defecations black as well. Nosebleeds last longer, thanks to it, and shaving cuts as well. It makes life somehow more heroic, escorting you to the brink of bleeder land even while propranolol conducts you down snoozy lane, where your extremities grow cold or numb, your response to cold intensifies, and your care for other people dwindles to the point of sublime callousness.

An Old Sweat

You soon become habituated to your symptoms, regarding them as old friends, or at least, in full phalanx, something as formidable and eidetic as the Palladium, the statue of Pallas on whose intactness the safety of Troy depended. For Pallas now read Star Wars. Most of all, of course, you become acquainted with death: how casual it can be, sidling in to claim you, just when you feel not half bad and think you are going to get away after all, you out of all those millions. I came close, I am told. I do recall seeing those who went into intensive care with me going out under sheets on gurneys, not in wheelchairs. I'll never forget watching how smoothly and omnipotently death operated in there, having its way with us almost at random, without any by-your-leave or warning or overture. It claimed and claimed without, I thought, even *wanting* any of us. It was just in the habit of taking us off. Death was a force with a tic. An eerie smoothness was among us at no one's request, something mathematical and implacable: no fuss, just naked universal power, the power that comes to mind (oddly, maybe) whenever I have to explain to someone the most puzzling part of my condition: my pacemaker remedies only the heart block otherwise known as sick sinus syndrome, it does nothing to curb arrhythmias; in other words, I am not going to keel over as Prokofiev did, unless my battery fizzles without warning, but I *am* going to feel sweaty and claustrophobic from time to time because the ventricles are beating chaotically. This very day, in fact, I was at a close-out sale, hunting short-sleeved shirts at seventy percent off (short-sleeved because they suit my condition, helping me feel a degree or two cooler). But the avalanche of lights, the jostling buyers, the high humidity, and the heat in there got me fibbing in no time at all and cut my shopping short.

I wanted out, indeed was consumed by the familiar and nerve-racking urge to be gone from there in a flash, away from the commotion. At such times I am hardly rational. People stare at the rivulets, at my matted and sodden hair, the nacreous patches of sweat on the front of my shirt. I look like someone fresh out of the shower. Giving a reading at the Cambridge Public Library in 1991, to a genial and attentive audience, I almost succumbed to the heat/humidity and the TV lights, but I sweated it out, mopping and wiping, yearning for a long blast from the air conditioner (it was near the microphone and had been switched off in the interests of quiet).

Since I first came to the United States, in 1952, as a student at Columbia, the air-conditioning in the city and the country has gone downhill. How fondly I remember the arctic bars of August; you entered, ordered, and dried off in no time, walking out with that exquisite brittle, starched feeling, and your nose cleared at last. Perhaps it is my illness that makes me think so, and the air-conditioning is as fierce as it ever was. People I mention this to respond both ways; but I, who from the sheer excitement of being in Manhattan need the severest artificial cool of all, almost the AC of the funeral parlor or the meat locker, think Americans have cut back to save energy. This used to be the coolest country in the world, and in those days we all needed it to be so. A cold beer had to have for its context an icy interior. Air-conditioning, I decided long ago, is like mercy; it brings me back to life when I am feeling drastically overcome, or overdone. When I can't get it, I lie in the bath covered (as nearly as possible) with ice cubes, as in Barbados once, or (as not so long ago in Paris) in deep cold water, marinating while the radio plays soothing music: in this case the afternoon program called "La Musique de l'Extase." Where else but in Paris. The spirit swoons with bliss while the carcass simmers. I have something in common with those people whose body thermostat is off. Occasionally I see someone perspiring brutally, and I know the cause more or less. So that is how I sometimes look, I think, and I know that, compassionate as I feel, the last thing that person wants is to be spoken to. An Old Sweat, I call myself, and it is always me you see badgering the flight attendant to have the crew turn up the air-conditioning. During a recent book tour lasting some five weeks, I lost fourteen pounds, all from toiling in the heat of an extraordinary late spring.

I hate clothing except for shirts and towels. I write naked, seated on a thick towel, and dread hats and neckties, suits and overcoats. My ideal garment is a leather construction apron made of heavy-duty split-suede leather, with five pockets and a breeze wafting through it. I have finally begun to know my body, too late perhaps to put it right, but in good enough time to treat it better, recognizing that the acrochordons (flesh tags) in my armpits are an index to hormone trouble, that the constantly splitting skin on my hands comes to me from my mother, that my sometimes inverted nipples reveal me as the migraine sufferer I used to be. I say hello to this stuff now, knowing I am going to have no other chemistry. Even my students have become used to my eyes, my hands swathed in Band-Aids, my crouch at the air conditioner even in winter.

There is a lethal context to all this wising up, which you get accustomed to, much as you get accustomed to the color of coreopsis or the rank aroma of narcissi. Your quiet mania says: After all that, I intend to get away with as much as I can for as long as I can; tread quietly and applaud my body for its ability to survive. Politicians talk of the art of the possible. Doctors talk about quality of life. I think about what my body achieved against the odds and what supports the rest of what I do: the art of the passable, and the high quality of that compared with the alternative. Death is no alternative to anything. I keep managing to come to the end of another chapter, say, and I marvel at the plenary gratitude the human spirit can feel after the Furies have had it by the short hairs and it has managed to slink away, back into the operating theater of words.

E T Y M O L O G Y
O F   N A T U R E

*I do not feel too bad about being a peerer, a starer,
an Autolycus, a ransacker, a browser, a starer-
down of dragonflies.*

Lion Dreams

One day, after talking about Marcel Proust, I sat
there at the seminar table and began to draw a plan
for a working model of Proust's own memory. I had
extolled his view of society as the well-to-do man's
toy, manipulating and re-creating at will; then his
view of memory (society's virtual complementary opposite) as something haphazard, not an instrument or
an act of will; and, finally, his view of prose, which
mediates between society and memory, making society mysterious and memory accessible. Now I was
envisioning something to be made with cogs and
rubber bands, wood and Scotch tape: a homemade,
Rube Goldberg thing whose very motions proved
Proust's point: You can't make memory serve you,

but, if you are lucky, without even trying, you can
entice it out. That, I discovered, was what I had been
doing in hospital, and ever after: lying there with an-
tennae ready, senses open, to receive the full comple-
ment of experience, not poking about after marvels,
but *almost* unwitting, expectant and not even eclectic.
I wanted it *all,* even what was lost to what Proust
called voluntary memory. I had a sense, I suppose, of
an event's shape: not of its most salient and dramatic
features only, but of the many tiny phenomena that
made it up and made it mine. Even if some of what
I thought it was happened to be imaginary, never
mind. I wanted to absorb the whole, musing on it as
one might rotate and contemplate an ancient jug,
identifying warp and texture. In the round, as we
planetarily say.

Would all of the TIA come back to me? Or of the
pacemaker's being implanted? The best preparation,
I decided, was to be unprepared, but always to be
alert. Most people, I thought, dealt with phenomena
in categories, naming a rough outline and then moving on; but I wanted the incidentals, the music off,
the atmosphere, the background radiation, resolved
to suck up the event as mine—yet without, as it were,
sucking up to it. So, after a while, instead of lapsing
into an event over with, it began to unhappen, rather
like the life reversed in Alejo Carpentier's story
"Journey Back to the Source," which moves from the
unbirth of death to the undeath of birth. It unpeels

back to its antecedents, to events that I never knew were going to be of any medical or creative significance. Lion dreams come back and assume their place in the conundrum of flesh. Stray words enter and rejoin other words. The event comes to resemble a poem once known by heart but mostly forgotten—a trite enough analogy, I know, except that, now, the poem has new words in it, and the text varies with each recollection.

It is 1914, and my father, a machine gunner in the Sherwood Foresters, is learning to eat army style, standing in line with his ration tin for a slice of bread dipped into simmering bacon fat. "Roll up for dip!" came the cry, and he counted himself lucky if he also got the thick caramel-like brew of tea thickened with condensed milk. He never lost the taste for dip and liked his eggs and bacon deep-fried in lard, always pouring molten lard onto his slices of white bread and—predictably—offering my sister and me delectable portions maneuvered to the side of his plate, for we flanked him while he ate, as if he were some kind of fairground exhibit. I remember seeing him cook for himself, drowning all in fat, perhaps because it made him feel at least as safe as he was in the war, when he had a machine gun to protect himself with. Unhealthy, of course, as we now smugly say; but I went on to develop similar tastes myself, long before the word "cholesterol" was known. Nothing tasted right unless it had been fried, and my palate—my chastened palate—still says the same, though it has learned to live with Pam. He choked his blood vessels, of course, and toward the end suffered much from atherosclerosis, which his son would one day discover came from the Greek word for "gruel." That was what the fatty plaque was like to the doctors who first examined it. We had a family habit too of smothering an unoffending slice of bread with best butter (as we used to say); ungreased it wouldn't go down, and we would sometimes smear it on pork pie, ham, and sausage. And the essence of a Yorkshire pudding's virtue was not so much the batter that composed it as the beef grease it had absorbed in the oven; after all, it began life as a substitute for meat, so the more it smelled like beef the better, even when beef was plentiful. Our eating was almost orgiastic. My mother, in those days, loved to down a pound of ice cream while quaffing a pint of stout. If we took in enough of what might kill us, perhaps we would domesticate death itself, daring it to accost us during the slow suicide whose corroded emblem was the frying pan. I am lucky to have got away with it; so were we all. We did not know that you are what you eat; we thought it just passed through you and left you as you always were.

I take some comfort in my memories of having always refused to eat fat, whether on ham, brisket, or bacon. I, Jack Sprat, could eat no fat, but I also spurned beets, greens, cheese, onions, pickles, and a whole range of other foods. A picky eater, I sometimes did myself some good, and I have come out the other end an eater just as picky, unable to face most raw fruit, and still those same onions and pickles. I hate yams and bagels, pea pods and cottage cheese. Perhaps, through the maze of my aversions, nature was trying to tell me something, but the good ideas remained smothered in refusals, most of which had no discernible basis in common sense, whereas my thwarted love of pineapple has one—it gives me canker sores that last a couple of weeks. I hear that it is possible to have too acidic a mouth to begin with, and I am not talking speech that wounds. I get by, eating as sensibly as I can manage, but pausing now and then to note the grain alcohol, the corn oil, and the propellant in Pam. Butter I gave up long ago, but margarine is just as perilous, as is the sweetness I dote on in the absence of liquor, tobacco, caffeine, and chocolate. I have become a fuddy-duddy of forbidden fruits, sticking to the cardiological menu, for the most part, but, like most of my friends on strict diets, now and then wandering off into a mindless, uncalculating spree in which the lethal significance of certain foods escapes me altogether. After I gave a reading at Washington University in Saint Louis, what should my gracious and generous hosts, Bill and Mary Gass, have for me but a huge chocolate cake? I tucked in,

telling the devil to take the hindmost. After all, it was
a rejoicing of prose stylists that evening, of the kind
that do not stint.

As for cutting calories, my worst experience has
been to live on seven hundred calories a day plus
three hours' swimming. I did that for three months
and in all lost five pounds. This way to heartbreak.
Soon after the TIA I was dieting well and managed
to lose twenty pounds each summer; but, gradually,
Inderal has quietened my metabolism so much that I
seem unable to burn anything off, no matter how
hard I swim. So I reassure myself that, losing little, I
nonetheless eat right—fake bacon, fake sausages,
fake egg, bread made of carrots (and, I think, sawdust). I have tried all the fake coffees too, from
Postum to Roma, the latter being quite the best of
those drinks made from beets (!), cereal, chicory, mo-
lasses, maltodextrin, and—I was going to say acorns,
mindful of the ersatz coffees of World War II, one of
the God-given punishments reserved for Nazi Germany. I wouldn't mind tasting a really good ersatz
coffee now and then, of a different breed: acorn or
horse chestnuts. I go to artificial sweeteners like a
bridegroom to his chamber, or at least as he used to
do in similes of an earlier generation. And, after
loathing yogurt, I now eat the iced and aerated va-
riety with relish while despising sherbets. As long as
it has plenty of sugar or sweetener in it, I will drink
almost anything prescribed, even the two-calorie diet

ginger ales and the one-calorie fruit drinks made from berries off bushes I have never heard of.

Something Neronic

Pill popping is a different matter, since there is no appetite requiring them. Many a shirt has come out of the dryer with a pale blue patch over the left-hand pocket from little twenty-milligram Inderals I forgot to remove from the seam into which they had carefully bedded themselves. No patch of blue seen by Oscar Wilde from Reading Gaol had more resonance and didactic shame than the patch-blotches on my shirts. I should not carry pills loose, but I keep on losing pillboxes, so I try to arrange little stashes of pills here and there. When I travel I keep my supply in a screw-top plastic jar that, over the years, has developed what I can only conclude is a miraculous internal dust from all the pills rattling together; a spoonful of that would quell any ill in short order and add punch to a fizzy drink. I should keep my pills separate, I know; but I can't face that much organization, so, the sublime dust apart, I have beta-blockers that regulate the heart a teeny bit while making me more of a bleeder, and bleed-provokers that curb the heart *and* slow it too. I play these games not in any spirit of defiance (though I am good at it), but because sometimes the full truth is too somber and I need that quiet pulverized miscegenation of the

drugs to feed my verbalist's cackle. It's the pharmaceutical equivalent of such a joke as: Where would
sarcastic people hold a roller derby? A scathing rink.
I was half in love with Inderal before I had to take
it, having bought my first *Physicians' Drug Manual*
secondhand and obsolete. There on page fifteen I discovered how many things Inderal was good for, including migraine, about which no doctor had ever
told me. Migraine prophylaxis, that is; it has no effect
on a gathering attack, for which there are other
drugs—but far better to fend it off than shoot it
down. In this same volume I learned *migraineur*,
evocative of *flâneur* (stroller) and *saboteur, bricoleur*
(handyman), and *voyeur*. A French intonation to one
of your diseases has a salutary effect.

It was Obeid's commonsensical humanity that, in
the days when I took the anti-arrhythmic, shifted me
from quinidine to Quinaglute, the difference being
that the former has to be taken four times a day, the
latter three, which translates into the difference between six and eight hours' sleep. I award the palm to
any doctor who honors sleep. We still understand little about sleep and dreams, but an entire profession
tramples through both in order to stick needles into
us at prescribed hours. Who knows what magical
seepage will not happen in the slumberer? Sleep I rate
just above Inderal, and, if I have to do an especially
difficult passage of prose, I try to sleep too much
beforehand—not seven or eight hours but ten or

twelve—and it works. Obeid and I agree on the eminent usefulness of both sleep and swimming; he gets too little of the first, he says, but he swims nightly after his duties end. He reads too little too, he says, but he has found time to work on a definitive text about echocardiography, which all echo-ologists will now have to read while he frees up his reading time again.

When first in hospital, I devoured my *PDM*, discovering that, on Coumadin, I might get priapism and urticaria: an itchy cocksman, to be sure, but also that henceforth I was to eschew leafy green vegetables (high in vitamin K), so goodbye, broccoli, spinach, cabbage, and cauliflower. What savorable irony: I had to wait decades for something to come along that would forbid me the foods I loathed. Reading these arcana of the medical profession sapped my fear a little. Like Kierkegaard, I was happy over seventy thousand fathoms, happy with the freakish phrasing (*thrombocytopenic purpura* is hemorrhage into the skin, mucous membrane bleeding, anemia, and low platelet count, whereas *thromboangiitis obliterans*— well, look it up for fun).

I was coming full circle, I felt, getting behind the scenes, learning the codes, flinching whenever medical embalmers created a compound word that combined a Greek with a Latin element: taboo among word builders, though seemingly okay among physicians. I felt like Admiral Canaris, the head of German counterintelligence, knowing all the local and distant secrets, even that a TIA might signal an impending major stroke. The heroic-sounding sympathomimetic agent was a drug able to mimic the actions of the sympathetic nervous system, and tardive dyskinesia (pure Milton,* this one) was uncontrolled movement, mainly of the face, lips, and tongue. It was like going to school again, learning to read the first two books of *The Odyssey* aloud in ten weeks and taking apart Latin poems whose words, because of Latin's suffixal rigor, could be recombined in only one way. I made up names of new diseases such as tardive tinnitus and murmured such new discoveries as Vincent's infection.

Educationally speaking, time to waste in hospital was of enormous value, restoring my veneration for dead languages (here they became hectically alive) and making me realize how the medical profession, in its Adamic way, had tidied almost everything up, naming and branding, honoring their most brilliant colleagues, making themselves freemen of a justifiable and concise taxonomy upon which all they had to do

---

*Milton's best coinage, Greek all through, was "Pandaemonium" (*Paradise Lost*, I.756). His word lasted; we needed it. His "ae" is the Roman version of Greek "ai." I once became so delighted with the growth of Milton's imagination that I wrote a novel about it, entitled *Sporting with Amaryllis*.

was build. I was sorry I wasn't a cardiologist, although later Obeid was to vow that he would make
one of me yet.

To be sure, there is something Neronic in all this;
the neurasthenic or the voyeur on the brink should
achieve a less restive peace. I never did, keeping myself busy to the sound of classical music that came in
on one of the blacked-out TV channels. No one
thought twice, *then*, about giving me caffeinated coffee, or lasagna, or pork sausages my father would
have left his urn for, provided he could regrease them.
Perhaps I thought cure came to the busy only; I have
a fidgety, though lyrical mind, trying always to
smooth heterogeneous or discordant experience into
a big, holistic swoosh. I had discovered the medical
and pharmaceutical world, and I wasn't about to
waste the tour, even if I wouldn't need it later on.
Something in me that loathes waste makes—made—
me fix on what doctors might think unconsiderable
trifles. I had again that old feeling of the scholarship
boy, the miserable specimen who lives only for examination day, thrilled to be alone with pen and paper for three hours, told to discuss the importance of
imagery to prose. In the old days I had tried to shine
at this, not so much arguing well as making my own
prose conspicuous, as unlike anyone else's as possible. Call it the narrow ecstasy. Such examinations are
less plentiful at Oxford and Cambridge than they

used to be, and the ways they have of weeding out young men are more prosaic. It was a show-off habit I never lost, however, and it matured into programmatic hedonism, which is one name for it, and hectic contemplation, which is another. The general way that people have of referring to phenomena—*The cow went into the square barn with a moo*—appeals to me not at all and sometimes causes me severe aesthetic distress. I am a microscope and telescope man, a demon of the magnifying glass. I want to know what I am among, and no generics. Hence my delight when, peering into my *American Heritage Dictionary*, I found that the quinine that stopped my blinking was almost the same as the quinidine that made my heartbeat regular. Here they are:

$$\text{Quinine:} \quad C_{20}H_{24}N_2O_2 \cdot 3H_2O$$
$$\text{Quinidine:} \quad C_{20}H_{24}N_2O_2$$

To my uninformed eye, that looks like a difference of three waters. I brought this gem of serendipity to Obeid, who gave me the look of the savant confronting the half-initiated infidel.

We are talking Quechua here too, as the "quin" comes from Spanish *quina,* meaning cinchona bark, short for *quinaquina,* which looks to me like five waters, not three, but is, of course, bark-bark. Two barks for three waters. What a kaleidoscopic intri-

cacy the world is, full of flukes swept up into the tide
of evolution and survival. Poring over its texture, as
reported in dictionaries and physicians' manuals, I
feel fortified, sustained, contented. I have become
privy to the etymology of nature itself; and, while I
hesitate to slap a "mystical" upon that experience, I
confess I do get a sense of unique and ravishing com-
plexity such as I get from a work of art, whether as
maker or appreciator. Suddenly there is no time. All
is harmoniously simultaneous within my head. The
walls are down. I hear that Cornell professors increasingly turn to Inderal to still the butterflies in
their stomachs when they make speeches, and I revel
in the contingency: what quells their stage fright
calms my heart. I have no stage fright at all, of
course, and no migraines either.

The tiny details remain with me, and the towering
structure that houses everything recedes a bit, too
vast not to be named something vacant, such as nature, meaning it once was *born,* an idea about which
there is now no argument. I have theories, but I take
courage from the fact that the word "theory" comes
from words less airy-fairy, such as *theōros,* meaning
"spectator," *theasthai,* "to observe," and *thea,* "a
viewing." It is almost as good as having three waters.
Before the theory, except for some Platonists and
mathematicians, there was the sense datum, so I do
not feel too bad about being a peerer, a starer, an

Autolycus, a ransacker, a browser, a starer-down of dragonflies. Perhaps that is why I miss the old migraines, those of blessed yesteryear, when, half the time, as I peered I saw only the process of my peering gone badly wrong.

PURE DELIUS

*I murmured my praises of all things bright and
beautiful, certain that a tiny slur in enunciation
from someone less than human would only earn me
tolerance in the swarming yard of summer.*

Suspended in the Web

In death's anteroom, with no plans made, I pored
over my *Physicians' Drug Manual* as if it were *The
Compleat Angler* of another species. I was becoming
increasingly a stranger to myself, whom I got to
know and sometimes to like. I sometimes liken this
experience or transit to the reader who can't accept
narrative without hearing about the extranarratorial
life of the narrator, or the narrator's feeling much the
same: needing to impose the details of his/her own
life on the reader, as if the attenuated convention
were no longer sufficient. I had become one of my
own characters, one who fought back and didn't
seem dependent on me, and who had somehow become emancipated from the duress of authorship and
didn't want to know about me anymore, no longer

wanted to stand in for me or be subject to my despotic whims. It's a weird feeling, exempting you from
answering when your name is called. An alias has
preempted you, enabling you to float out into the gal-
axy, where you have no significance at all. I was a
bully boy in those days, quite brave, I thought, as if
intensive care were only some coda to being bombed
by the Nazis, when my father and I would wander
outside to watch the searchlights, with brisket sandwich in hand, listening to the patter of falling shrap-
nel. Something just as foolhardy and just as defiant.
I am not so sanguine now, having spent my last ten
years trying to behave as a normal man when I knew
all along that I was straining, pushing, getting out of
character.

The shift or transit from intensive to intercare I
have already mythicized so much that I scarcely know
the facts anymore. It was magical, at midnight, and
I was just settling down. Either a vacancy had oc-
curred or my bed was needed. Or, believe it or not,
both. The arrival of the nurses was stealthy enough,
perhaps to get me away while I was asleep; but I saw
them make sure nothing got left behind and, a bit
groggy in my wheelchair, rolled on rubber along hallways and into elevators, wondering if there would be
a TV at the other end. IC had been quite dim, billowy
with sail, and several times I thought about the time,
on a platform, with microphone, when I asked Jorge
Luis Borges his favorite word. After a long, ferreting

pause, that was the word he said. *Dim.* He saw the joke. I was not ready for the big scoops of light at my destination. There was a barrier, as at immigration, and I had the strongest sense that Lord Tennyson was there, presiding, lest there be any moaning at the bar. One nurse, freshly laundered and shampooed, with an extraordinary foreign name only James Joyce would have thought up—something like Aguilar des Roncevalles-Chamonix—welcomed me, and I knew I had died on the way over. It was all so dazzling, wholesome, scrubbed, with several nurses gleaming in starched white and jangling gold: white, samite, mystic, wonderful, the words my mother and I used to intone together when I was little and we were having one of our Tennyson sessions. They greeted me like a war hero, fussing me with slippers, robe, pajamas, a new little set of ablution vessels (mug, bowl, tray, comb, toothbrush), no longer contaminated by the atmosphere of the charnel house. I had crossed the date line, that was it. I was being glad-handed by the light militia of the lower sky. There would be medals tomorrow. These were streamlined, bosomed nurses, better dressed than the death-handlers in IC, and they smiled, they fawned, they chortled. I was the novelty of their night, amazed to be using my voice again for trivial things. Tomorrow I was going to be allowed a shower and shave. I saw my face in the bathroom mirror and recoiled from that shaggy mutant, wondering how the nurses had been able to be genial, glad to have *me* among them. I was alive, that was why; they loved a live one rolling toward them from the never-never, cowering from the lights and asking daft questions. No, they told me, I would have a companion, who was recovering from a stroke too, but a curtain would separate us if we wished it. Thank God, I thought, I have my little radio. For an event such as this they should be playing Walton's First Symphony, full of plangent twisting exultation tempered with shrill misgivings, or Busoni's piano transcriptions of Bach, all euphoric clang and bright defiance.

This was recovery number one, whereas the recovery after pacemaker implantation was a slight thing (I had asked for a turkey sandwich as soon as I got back to my room, and got one too). I must have been feeling better, or enormously lifted by the change of venue: I at once asked for a private room with a telephone and a view of something summery (it was August still). They took this as a good sign and, after a bit of bureaucratic shuffling on the next day, obliged. The poor devil in the next bed had still not regained his speech or his legs, but he was no longer at death's door; we chatted as best we could, and I realized this was his second stroke, slap-bang while he was recovering from the first. He must be tough, I thought; he's tougher than I am. So, for a while, he got the room to himself, and the custodial graces of Aguilar et cetera as well. It comes to me now, after all this time: those nurses had tans.

I slept little that night, too excited at the thought of beginning to get well. Here there was no chute down which to slither after being wrapped, no floaty curtain through, past, which to go in a terminal flurry. In those hours of darkness, as I waited for the sun to come up (in which I had a renewed interest), I began to take stock of my body, its still useless left arm, the almost wholly retracted penis scared back into the body cavity, the crudely shaved chest, the swollen right arm from a misplaced heparin needle that had bloated the muscle. I twiddled my toes against the stiff wrapper of the sheet, wrinkled my nose, blinked. It had been a surprising day and night, almost like getting a new illness. I had been in intensive care a week. My mother knew nothing of the truth, only that I had had a migraine and kept going to the hospital for weekly tests.

"Not just one attack," she said observantly. "One after another."

"The usual," I said, "plus a bit extra. I'll cope."

"Do you have Paramax there?" she asked, naming the drug she herself took. We did not. "How backward America is," she teased. "I could tell them all about it."

Oddly enough, with my blood pressure lowered for perhaps the first time in my life, I felt quite good, although weak. I began to concentrate, as I do even now, on the salient moments—the arrivals and departures—rather than on the curative processes in between, or the balsa-legged marches to the maternity ward and back, or the first full-length bath in an enormous room empty of all else.

Suspended in the web of chemistry, I began to yearn to go home; I had not wanted to before, somehow convinced that I would never go there again.

The Furies

Released at last, after three weeks, I wanted to hug the whole late summer, having forgotten how green and distended it could be, how thick and noisy. I half remembered another immersion in nature, from the Arizona Inn, when late at night I had stepped out of bed and put my feet into an assembly of crickets that had come from behind the skirting board and taken over the soft green rug. Arriving late at the inn, in fog, we had been told with manicured regret that our room was not available, as someone had stayed on, but would we accept instead something a little different, across the road. Away we went to "House 6," which turned out to be a three-bedroom villa with three patios, a lawn, fireplaces galore with mesquite logs already in place. What style, we thought, mentally boosting the Arizona Inn to the top of our sybarite list. That arrival had something in common with the two arrivals I am recalling: unwonted, invalidating, making you learn a new idiom fast, become a new member of a different race. The late August of 1984 was my own special orgy of chlorophyll; I had glimpsed it from my window as I peered at Route 13, going up the hill that led to home. But, becoming vaguely aware of it that Sunday afternoon while going in search of a blood pressure machine, I felt myself heating up in response to it, to its costiveness, its stoked-up-ness, its big abundant impersonal swilling about, with everything in place: no twig, no bloom, no bird being unorthodox, but all according to the old formula I had forgotten about while being processed and primped. I was in two minds again: on the one hand, jubilant that life was not all processes, all in-betweens, but sufficiently peppered with events; on the other hand, worried that, precisely because of events, there would never be enough stable continuum. What did I want? Peak or trough? I wanted all, in a greedy impromptu ravening that excluded my major vices. "This weekend," Obeid had said, "have your last cigar, your last cognac. Make a ritual of it." I made a ritual of everything else as well, relearning color and sound: the snail-track silvers in the crust of the shagbark hickory, the muted steady note of the catbird and its overstated silences. For a week I did nothing save sit there humped, staring at summer's routine surplus, then having a long swim, after which I stared again, copied the birdcalls and sang them as high as I could go, only to reproduce them quite well as whistles. Back in the world of air conditioners, postage scales, shortwave radios, typewriters, and Touch-Tone phones, I gave thanks to nature for red things, elastic things, things that sparked and funneled; for juices, slops, pastes. I learned the discipline of pill taking and, one morning, after too much Inderal prescribed, fell over sideways, lucky not to crack my head. In warm pool water I felt overcome. If I craned my head backward, I almost fainted. I had a permanently dry mouth, numb fingers, cold toes, and a slight distortion in my speech, a Lilliputian twitch in my lower right lip. These were my secrets, between me and the Furies. I murmured my praises of all things bright and beautiful, certain that a tiny slur in enunciation from someone less than human would only earn me tolerance in the swarming yard of summer. The mood was pure Delius.

That Pink Leak

Once again I am fifteen, playing soccer in the freezing rain, feeling a numbness cut through me, landing up in the bone marrow. I develop a fever and spend months in bed, coughing into an enamel bucket, delirious on and off, and dreaming that an enormous cloud of snow is choking me, smothering me. It is before antibiotics, of course. I recover, but am unable to walk, and my first outing is like that after three weeks in bed with the TIA. When you feel this flimsy, this faint, you know the forces arrayed against you are indomitable, and you want to give in, tame as a sheep, mindless as frog spawn. The same youth was born too late in his mother's life, and he began to dote on works of art because his body kept failing him, even though he shoved it into jockery. If, say, that buzzing in the lips of 1984 had arrived sooner, he would have acquiesced in becoming an invalid, blinded by his first migraine at eleven.

What was it, I wonder, that gave me the impetus to fashion a lifestyle; a chalice in the sump? What urged me to literature and music? It must have been my mother, who went through enormous pain—having her womb tilted to and fro—in order to have me. Migraine and gallstones dogged her all her days, and arthritis; she downstared angina at fifty, pounding onward for art, for music. I genuinely think what brought me through was the prospect of tougher tests, intellectual mainly, and I compare then with now, noting that now I have loads of intellectual energy but not much physical; on no stimulants, I am chatty and chipper for lunch but go downhill smoothly thereafter, and I am adequate for lunch only because I rise at noon. The day's big demand begins at midnight, and I write for as long as I can, with the planet stilled, the vibration down. I must be fooling myself if I think I am up to more than six hours a day of anything, close to something like nar-

colepsy for the rest of it. Yearning for rebirth, as in
Arizona, where I wondered at first what was missing,
and it was humidity; I could breathe for the first time.
My mother had pneumonia when she was nineteen,
and all her hair fell out. When it grew back, a paler
brown, it was to stay with her forever, never to go
gray. I think of that as a rebirth, as I do of my father's
getting his sight back after being blinded in 1917.

How does it go, my little litany of prevalence? Because I am still able to write my books, to teach, and
give readings, I develop uncanny high spirits: a horn
of plenty of cheer, which I think surprises those who
know me. Underneath, though, I feel the old immo-
bilized panic, the drooped eyelids of the stroke, the
slurred speech. I have been mortified into becoming
some *Homo adaptatus,* a modified man, as if I had
grown a metal empennage to fly with. I need a steady
diet of exemptions: flying with painter Steve Poleskie
in his Piper Apache at five hundred feet along the
shore of Lake Cayuga, from Ithaca to Fair Haven, to
survey sharp-sliced cliffs that look as if Wyndham
Lewis had been let loose there with a sandblaster. I
need to be in the St. George's Club, Bermuda, staring
at the grass for hours while the yo-yo at the center
of my head cools down and the sleek, impassive high
of the beta-blocker begins. I need my vocal cords to
do nothing for three hours while I aurally inspect the
silence. I dream dreams of a boyhood never had.
Stranded in inspiration, I sit writing by the air con-

ditioner to the music of Gerald Finzi. Working on a
long book, I wash my glasses in detergent halfway
through, and that is the extent of my mechanical
skills. As my hair comes out on the brush, I save it
in an envelope to make a wig with, or a skullcap such
as André Gide wore to keep his lustful head toasty.
There are certain benefits too. Since I am part bionic,
I can take as much Inderal as I want ("as needed," it
says on the box); my pacemaker will always keep the
heart beating at the right rate. Otherwise the drug
would slow it to a crawl. My blood test is monthly
now: almost an endearing rite, which it was not when
weekly. My legs are strong, honed by swims, except
for flickers of sciatica that only extra swimming
seems to quell. I can do a lot for myself in that pool,
acquiring, as I grandly announce, even more muscle,
which weighs heavy. I am all muscle, I say, but those
dear to me jeer and accuse me of writing fiction. Only
in the pool, where I am a mere fraction of what I
usually weigh, do I lose weight. I have become something of a comic. A flight in a piston-engined plane
gives me the shakes for a day; it must be the vibration; I go anyway. I still think my basilar artery is
wrong, but no one finds anything. If, Diane says, you
got up soon after dawn, when I do, I would see more
of you. No, you wouldn't, I say, I'd be asleep all afternoon. I can't work in the day anyway; the phone
rings all the time. I think art should be surreptitious,
like being at the movies. I see the dawn each writing

day, and remember how my father was always up at six to watch it, that pink leak. The birds hail it, but I get an infernal hankering never to sleep again, always being suckered into the open by the vermilion, the birds, the breeze, the rumble of the first plane out.

Flutter Vertigo

Morning, as I facetiously call it, is a dangerous time for someone such as me. Cardiologists warn you about swinging out of bed and getting cracking just when your beta-blocker level is low; your quinidine too. Most strokes and heart attacks happen at this time, I'm told; so, if I get the chance, as when I wake an hour early, I take my pills to boost the levels, and then I arise suitably dosed. As it is, when I wake, the visual world is ashake with flutter vertigo and remains so for half an hour. It is also important at this time to get some food aboard, a suggestion I have never been known to fight. It still takes me a couple of hours to feel awake, though I can handle phone calls soon after rising, as if the trousers press in my skull is working independently of my waking tantrum. No coffee, of course. So what? I'm lucky to be alive, on two legs, able to complain. The most demoralizing thing of all is to get up, at last to wake up, and then succumb to an urgent craving for sleep. A seminar or a workshop will usually bring me to my senses, but right after it I have to get my head down to rid my being of that grotesque feeling: a drained, stammering, blanched tremulousness that recalls what the neighbors used to call me when I was little: Pale Paul.

After my one- or two-hour nap, I feel as if someone altruistic has rinsed my brain, stroked my membranes, polished my eyes. The change is extraordinary, and I feel none of that hung-over stuff other nappers complain about. I feel new, reprieved, purged, only partly stoked up, however, and itchy about wasting so much time. I should know better; I know what the trade-offs are. But I hate feeling helpless, half baked, a bit of an encumbrance, who doesn't drive (I think of myself as a New Yorker). I am not young enough, or light enough, or enough of a Type B; I am sometimes almost ready to donate my body to science as an anthology of no-no's. Then somebody like Stanley Elkin, blasted by MS, looks at me (this happened) and says: We're the same age. Look at you. Look at me. He sees a whited sepulcher, though; my crutches or stilts are internal, as indeed are some of his. Oh, he doesn't look so bad, really; he is just kidding, dissimulating how much he respects himself in spite of everything.

Having survived, I think sometimes of two old friends who never called to ask my condition: not once, during several months, and I marvel at such exquisite severance. They know who they are, but they don't know the comparative strangers who did call. I forgive them, in my bearish way; they were afraid of death by proxy, not of me, and they were both fading out anyway. You cherish those who came closest, sneaking into the tent of the leper to gesticulate succor: a poet, a pilot-painter, an historical novelist, a science writer, an astronomer. These are the true maintainers of the body beautiful, its accomplices and helpmeets. You do not expect them to come see you, for you associate doors with curtains that flow easily past you as your packaged carcass rolls through, headed for the basement; but they come anyway, a bit cowed by the freak in the bed, the stewards in white or candy stripe, the smell of—what is that unique hospital stench? Feces plus carbolic plus rotting celery. Is that even close? Something is going off, you know, and you want your visitors to hold their breath for the full half hour, after which they are free to retch in the elevator or the parking lot. I had more phone calls from fans than from fellow novelists, and I kept remembering the novelist, well known for it, who when someone did well always looked him or her up to see who was older. If older, then okay. I imagined this time-tried fellow looking me up, finding I was a fraction older, and then letting his mind relax as one of the old guard slid down his plank into the sea.

If you manage to survive a stay in hospital, and some do not, the net result is sanative: you discover that all these hygienic people are, as you, engaged in the commonplace enterprises of life: fellow fumblers, with piles, acne, and aerophagia. Not a breed apart, although you will not harm them much if something goes wrong with you; that is when they string you like a bead on the line of incorrigible loss, fast-waning from a memory into a blur.

THE
INTERROGATING
BEAM

It is like hearing Sir Thomas Browne and an outstanding trumpeter or railroadman in the same breath.

Mosaic Tablet

Eight years after my TIA, I was in hospital again, for the third time. An abscess in my rear had plagued me all through a symposium in Buffalo. I left early, flew to Syracuse, and Diane delivered me to the emergency department. I was in appalling pain, unable to walk or sit, but I soon got relief; during the initial examination, the abscess burst. And the next day it burst again, swilling blood down my legs as I stood there in my shift. A group of nurses watched as blood pooled around my naked feet, hypnotized by the sight of a man having a heavy period. Finally someone threw in the towel, and I felt relief, although trussed up in sanitary pad and yards of sticky tape.

This, I kept musing, was the hospital where Obeid used to do rounds, proclaiming the virtues of sleep. His patients needed to dream as well. He no longer came near, however, but one of his deputies did, a man more committed to insomnia—and with whom I was to have unfortunate dealings. Once again I watched the despotic indifference of hospitals to the patient's peace of mind. Awakened every two or three hours for tests, I mustered enough presence of mind to notice my medications were being delivered late, and in the wrong amounts. My Coumadin dose was only half what it should have been, and I was being fed generic Quinaglute—bad news because some patients had died through generic Quinaglute's having been biologically unavailable. They got enough, only too late.

Somebody fetched the head nurse, or at least the *Gauleiter* of that particular medical *Gau*. I complained, reciting what I had learned about the cardiological perils of awakening. At once she needed beta-blocker to calm her as she launched into a tired tirade against know-it-all patients who brought their own medications into hospital. That wasn't the issue, I told her; I'd come straight from a plane anyway. The thing that bothered me was wrong dosage, wrong time. She had never heard about the dangers of generic Quinaglute, spelled out for me with altruistic dedication by Peter, one of two local pharmacists I admire (Hank the other, the book lover). Peter had also counseled me about the poisons self-administered by Dr. Polidori in my novel *Lord Byron's Doctor*. Obeid's deputy, sent for, failed to appear, but he sent a fax of the Mosaic tablet from on high. The hospital, he had told the head nurse to tell me, did not exist "for the convenience of patients"—a fatuous phrase in which, in this case, "convenience" had to mean "safety" or even "life preservation." All I had wished to do was fend off a statistically likely stroke or attack while my body labored away under the affront of medication hours late. Indeed, my sedulously observed regimen had gone by the board; I was getting three medications at haphazard times, and the exquisite pacing prescribed by Obeid no longer applied. *Of course* I was fibrillating, and of course my blood pressure kept going up, and of course, on only half the usual dose of Coumadin, my blood was that much nearer to clotting. I was close enough to severe trouble to make a row, and I made it. At last the surgeon who had examined my abscess and presided over its demise, a genial man with a passion for speaking Italian and recommending Barbados, apologized for his colleague. Obeid, when told what had been said, dismissed the whole episode as a juvenile exercise in irony, but I didn't buy that euphoric bit of whitewash, and he knew it. A hospital so lackadaisical and uninformed had no

right to power of life and death over anyone. I mused
that, even in the humdrum temples where literature
gets "taught" and a mulled aroma of fatigue and disappointment wafts along the hallways, such indifference might just have brought a severe reprimand, and
that in a sphere where mortality was no threat. It is
surely not in the patient's best interests, when struck
down by something fierce, to have to monitor the
doings of experts. Must the wounded witness examine the bungling savants? Apparently so. I had known
a good many medical students at several universities,
and they had none of them struck me as any more
devoted to healing or intellectual rigor than those
specializing in literature, sociology, or math. If teach-
ers of literature wore white coats and carried steth-
oscopes, would students trust them more? I am not
alone, I think, in having spent anxious hours brooding on the servile, subordinate, blind deference one is
supposed to achieve in the presence of men and
women in white. I still find it hard to believe a deputy
cardiologist sent me the message that a hospital is run
for other reasons than the patient's convenience, well-
being, peace of mind. (Undergraduates at famous research universities lodge a similar complaint: that
teaching takes a back seat; but a university is not
a hospital, not yet anyway.) We patients must recognize we are secondary to research (presumably
knowledge for the sake of knowledge), tidy admin-
istration, and the play of absolute power. We are sup-

posed to look after ourselves. How many tyrannical oafs does a hospital need before it dwindles into incorrigible uselessness? Entering the damned place is like going blindfold into Indian country. My shock came, of course, from having dealt with Obeid for so long. He would no more have sent such a message than he would have lauded doctors who need more than two hundred thousand a year. So it became a hospital *minus him,* with sleep slandered and precise life-delivering regimen thrown to the wolves. The meal service was much more punctual than the pill wagon.

The Invisible Riviera

Pondering all this, I learned that in addition my blood glucose was up to eight hundred; I was a diabetic, and something had to be done about it. They would keep me there and test me relentlessly, but I was in no mood to be messed with. I'd had a small stroke; I had a pacemaker in my chest; I had atrial fibrillation, anyway, and labile blood pressure, and now I had another brand on me. Suddenly the meals became dry, tiny, and inedible; I was to lose weight. Well, if so, I wasn't going to lose it in there.

Encouraged by one doctor who said the blood sugar would probably go down even farther as the abscess drained, I had them let me go, promising I would eschew sugar, as I do. My problem is not so

much that I need insulin as that my body is loath to
use the insulin I have. Exercise helps, and so does
aspartame. I have all the classic symptoms, from
fungi and incessant thirst to weight loss, from
cracked heels to blurred vision (now diminished). Diabetes is the great aggravator, making already exist-
ing conditions worse, especially cardiac and dental
ones. Worst of all, as Obeid says, the things that
boost my blood pressure will also raise my blood
sugar. Stress, for instance; so I try to remain twice as
calm as before, cultivating an uncallous quietude, a
mellow exuberance.

I have bad days several times a year, when I cannot
be bothered to find out what it is that's acting up. I
just assume it's everything and duck out of sight, listening to the favorite music (carefully assembled on
CDs) that Proust enjoyed: the Franck quartet, Fauré's
Piano Quartet in G minor, Debussy's quartet, and
others. Swallowing so much music without reading
at the same time, I embark on a voyage far beyond
the wayward and punitive regimes of hospitals. It
would be best, if possible, to listen while swimming,
as I sometimes do when quite well. But to swim
while fibrillating isn't much fun, so I make Proustian
plunges between the sheets, creating my own hospital
bed of consummate harmony. Sometimes Diane will
come and stroke my chest, exerting upon me something like magnetic osmosis (my stroking a cat or a
dog might produce the same effect, but a distin-

guished poet is a far more magical accomplice). Clearly, a great deal is up to me, to us. After writing for two or three hours (never more), I float off to the land of inconsequence by watching movies so vacant they remind me of aviation jargon for when the skies are "severe clear": CAVU, meaning "ceiling and visibility unlimited." I have come to prize this variant of feedback, when the eerie chemical peace of the beta-blocker fuses with the cadenced telepathy of Franck, Fauré, Debussy, and Ravel. There is a slow, purposeless wafting away. I go boneless. All of my various conditions or states become the same, the good along with the bad. I feel proud of myself, having smuggled my body into serenity. Lucky to have taught myself how to do this trick, I lower both blood pressure and glucose level. It is like being freed from all the gravities while being slid into trances that are cool and complete. It is the invisible riviera of the visible world.

Does it always work? Is the IR always open? No, but the universe itself doesn't always work too well. Whatever this thing is, it works better for me than my engineer father's metal lattices—though I ogled them greedily when he sketched them on blueprint paper—but no better than my pianist mother's crackling forays into theory and harmony. The music side is clearly coming forth. Fluid autonomy, I sometimes call the state I enter. Or vicarious autology, not immune to mishaps vascular or pancreatic, but lofted far from them to the point at which they dare not enter the lists. Or, if they do, only with a shamefaced pedantry. *Leave me alone,* I murmur; *listen to Franck, Fauré, and Co.* In this state, prompted no doubt by memories of Proust's buying for his lover Agostinelli the plane in which Agostinelli died, I dream about my favorite planes. Fred Weick's Ercoupe you can slow up by opening the side window and planting your palm firmly on the wing while your passenger does the same on the other side. The Bellanca Viking has a mahogany plywood wing that has sliced through telephone poles. And the Mooney 201 has that forward-slanted tail, as if the plane were being blown along from behind. In these I overfly the Sonoran desert. West the novelist takes over and sends me places that did not exist until I lay down to soothe myself. All this drifting and wafting never leads to drooling, but I know I am a ripe specimen for those who teach music therapy. Literature has no such effect at all, although, visibly, literary music has uncanny power.

Echo Chambers

Although Obeid no longer stalks the halls of the hospital, he is even more of a presence, this time in print. The definitive study he has been working at for years, *Echocardiography in Clinical Practice,* has been published, including many color plates that show how ultrasound passes through body tissues having different densities and different "acoustic impedance." Having had the electric transducer applied to my chest, I have some idea of what he means when he writes the following in his introduction:

> At the interface of tissues with different acoustic impedance, some of the incident energy is reflected and the rest continues until it meets another boundary. The reflected signals carry the information that is harvested in echocardiography.

Heart echoes are what he "harvests": echoes of big structures such as valves, pericardium, and ribs. Color Doppler echocardiography, however, targets blood cells and gives a colored image depending on the speed and direction of the blood's flow. It can also pick up platelets and white blood cells. The principle, I understand, is that, as reflected ultrasound signals shift frequency, their color changes. It is just as if we were looking at stars, as Christian Johann Doppler was in the nineteenth century. Stars coming toward us exhibit a blue shift; those going away, a red one. Blood approaching shows blue; blood going away shows red. You can see the changes in a diagram of what looks like a plumber's joint, but mimics the ascending and descending aortae. Fast blood in the ascending aorta shows yellow, then red, brown, blue, pale blue, and green. From such basic effects come the complex color Doppler plates scattered throughout the book, though Obeid counterpoints them with photographs of a more familiar type, such as one of clots evacuated from a pulmonary artery "at emergency embolectomy"—one battered-looking earthworm together with a worm coiled into a bloated ring, and a worm chopped up. That is what this layman sees, clinging to familiar appearances like a realist afraid of the abstract.

Indeed, I look at these astounding pictures with little sense of personal intimacy; they could be pictures of my own heart, for all I know, at least until I read the captions. I am more impressed that this used to be the kind of view you could not get until postmortem. Now it comes twinkling out of the body on demand, a chromatic cardiological fingerprint, a freeze-frame of incalculable medical usefulness. Similar to "windows" into space, to the gorgeous color plates sold commercially by little shops annexed to huge telescopes, the color Doppler echo is both cool candor and holy emblem. You do not have to rip the chest apart to get it, and the experience of being transduced is actually quite soothing. You can watch and marvel. Hypnotized by Obeid's page 194, I stare at those earthworm-like bits of blood and slowly let my gaze move upward to the plate: "A 23-year-old female with sudden onset of respiratory distress post partum." White arrows denote "A large serpiginous clot . . . in the right atrium across the tricuspid valve and coiling in the right ventricle." "Serpiginous" means creeping, and, if you look carefully, you can see the elliptical clot and its spiral down. Thus, in the one shot, the clue; in the one below, the gunk cut out. I try to join the two versions in my mind's eye, wondering if the upper plate (black and white) would have made a better match had it been in color. But no, it was not blood cells moving, was it? It was congealed blood resembling meat and therefore a target for routine echocardiography only. Artist that I am, I want the most from my senses, resentfully thinking how Obeid and all scientists use the word "artifact" to mean an undesirable, erroneous effect. But Obeid, much as he seems one, is not the medieval monk of the heart, coloring it in, *illuminating* it, as if it were a huge initial capital; he is a heart inspector, a transcendental plumber intent on lifesaving data. My fiction, he tells me, reminds him of Wagner, which I take as a compliment, so I must not saddle him with inappropriate similes. Very well: he is a cardiological astronomer such as Doppler never dreamed of.

Indeed, against his will, he is an image maker, a phrase maker, evoking notions in my mind that match few in his. He writes about "smoky echoes," "biplane probe," "tumor blush," "aliasing," "poppet," "single gate," and "flail," sending my imagination on a merry chase that ends when I tell him that what he calls the "suprasternal notch" used to be called the heart-spoon. He's pleased that some-

times our jargons meet and mesh. Amazed and a bit
put out when I rattle off my verbal findings to him,
he doesn't see the Joycean fun I have with "poppet,"
say, and I realize that both he and most scientists
regard verbal play as irresponsible. Is it any more
irresponsible, though, than telling the person operated upon that medicine is not an exact science? Is it
any more irresponsible than telling the patient *that* is
devious? Doctors pride themselves on dealing with
life and death, but offer their best interventions as
works of art. Yet we, who give the word "artifact"
its true dignity, do not appropriate, say, "aliasing"
and make it mean one doctor hiding behind another.
Perhaps we should, as the need mounts, and the Ma-
sonic sodality of the profession thickens.

All such striving pales in the presence of Obeid's
heavy textbook: those snapshots of masses, tumors,
clots, vegetations, valves, pericardia, and shunts,
which last I imagine I have seen floating on the surface tension of swimming pools—pine needles elon-
gated and narrow, like fully retracted umbrellas,
ready to be slid into the blood vessel to halt clots.
Dipping into his album, you sample histological biography, leafing from "a 60-year-old patient with a
bio-prosthesis in the mitral valve position" to "a
patient with transposition of the great vessels after
atrial switch repair." It is like hearing Sir Thomas
Browne and an outstanding trumpeter or railroadman in the same breath. Paging through, I wonder at

the terse summary to which an entire lifetime's com-
plexity can bring us (or a child's bad luck). Each picture is a short story implied. "Two days after therapy
with streptokinase. The flow profile through the tricuspid valve now shows a much wider jet. . . ." Imagine the relief. In another shot, however, a straight
arrow points to an anterior mitral leaflet that "must
have been damaged accidentally during surgery."
Imagine the chagrin. I am almost ready to dream
when I read: "Mitral regurgitation is seen in tur-
quoise in the lower panel (open arrow)" and "This
ultrasound emanates from valve closure that triggers
the crystals and is not a reflected echogenic signal."
Reading such matter, perhaps a novelist should try
to work backward from the cardiological data to the
life lived, guessing, imagining, presuming, wondering
how the patient walks, eats, dreams. An ace echo-
cardiologist might be able to imagine your echocar-
diogram in detail after studying your disease and
your lifestyle. Maybe novelist and doctor would run
into each other in some advanced stage of divining
surmise as the one finds the personality in the echo,
the other the echo in the personality. I doubt it, but
the pipe dream makes better friends of us. Perhaps
laypersons who flinch from the bald recital of epit-
omes—Starr-Edwards (ball-in-cage) valve prosthesis;
Ebstein's anomaly; Konno's procedure: the honor roll
of the discipline become a catalogue of woes and
fixes—are right, and it is merely morbid to tinker

with the eponymous quirks of a healing profession. I go the other way, snapping up unconsidered (or highly prized) trifles all the way, from Fibropapilloma to Effusive Disease, reminded by Obeid's book that nothing should be alien to me. Any one of his color plates, minus its arrows and legends, would make a handsome sample of abstract art, say a Kandinsky-Dufy-Ensor. Thus the revenge of the artifact, taking the doctors by surprise as the perfect image of nature's work becomes a subjective or an accidental abstract.

It reassures me to have Obeid's classic beside me: not only all this evidence of his expertise, but his prose, his arguing voice. I know that he has foresuffered all this already, and is ready for more. Master of what he names "the interrogating beam," he is at his tightest, curtest, here; but although I know his book is a compendium of misery and pain, I see something therapeutic in its order, its poise. The Faustian-Promethean side of me warms to his desire to get it right, to put it right, to figure it all out, to pass on the data to successors. Where would so many of us be without his echo, with enigmatic chests awaiting the saw? I revel in these sneak previews of the pathologist's wares. Mostly, it is a live human that answers the interrogating beam, atremble and ablaze, no doubt, but responsive still. And it is only poetic justice that the beam's exquisite finitudes also confront us with, as a by-product, a shower of colors, a parade of lolling triangles full of snow and autumn leaves, blue sky and old-fashioned red blood. Sure enough, it is the heart translated, not altogether recognizable, but glossed and explained, even if what you see looks more like a tepee than like tricuspid regurgitation, a white lupine than a large sessile mural thrombus. Imaginatively misreading these images, and relishing unique patterns of color, I am in a way sapping the damage on show of its horror, and the heart of its potential for harm. Taking liberties, I discover a new pageantry with a quaint argot all its own: not, surely, the words a heart might have come up with if literate, but some cordial prolongation of the beam that shines all the way from the ancient Greeks and the Romans to Obeid the Arab. Sessile is Latin. Mural too. Thrombus is Greek. Does he ever wonder that so few medical terms are Arabic? Astronomy is full of Arabian words and names. Myself, I wonder if medicine has more Greek than Latin words; but the comparison will prove pointless, as many Greek words became Roman ones.

Passionate hobbyist of my own illness, I ponder such matters in much the same spirit as I memorize the names of all the actors when a movie's final credits roll—not because I care who they are, but because I want to show myself I am still competent. Unaware that it will soon vanish, I watch the Sunday medical channel on TV, awed by how crisp and scrubbed the cardios look, how happy with their mystery. Then I remember that cardiology has advanced farther in the last ten years than any other branch of medicine. It has soared ahead, much lowering the numbers of those who succumb to heart disease. Better to have this than cancer, I muse: there are so many ways to go, unless you have sudden death or congestive heart disease. Obeid has taken me off Quinaglute, whose notorious laxative properties did no more than keep me blissfully regular. It is one of the anti-arrhythmic drugs thought dangerous, though not as dangerous as encainide, moricizine, and flecainide, the last of which Obeid had considered using on me. Such drugs have more or less been withdrawn, except from pa-tients with arrhythmias that can cause fainting spells and our old friend, sudden death, spoken of so gently it almost sounds benign. Speaking of Quinaglute, Obeid became quite witty, suggesting my dose was more homeopathic than therapeutic. No more tinni-tus. No more regularity. I miss that old pill, best taken, says my *Physicians' Desk Reference*, with an adequate amount of fluid, "preferably in an upright position, to facilitate swallowing." Yes indeed: it won't go down, nowhere near smooth enough to glide. Quinaglute was always tricky, since the thera-peutic and the lethal dose were not far apart. There was never much room for maneuver.

"I have," I told Obeid one day by telephone, "a rather anthropomorphic-sounding question. Now I'm off Quinaglute, are we asking too much of Inderal?

Now it's not only lowering my blood pressure, it's soothing and slowing the heart. I've noticed that my blood pressure's been going much higher than usual, maybe from the demands made of the drug. So I increased the dose from sixty milligrams three times daily to eighty. That seems to work. Was that okay?" Of course, he said, reminding me that I am to take the drug *as needed*. Get the pressure down at all costs. If I slow my heart too much, the pacemaker will kick in. I sometimes forget I have a partly artificial heart. I go on wondering how much good the Quinaglute was: reassuring, no doubt, but perhaps in the end no more than well-meant trifling. To call it Quinny, as I sometimes did, was to mark its slightness, though I intended no such thing, was just befriending my elixirs; Inderal has often enough been Indy, sometimes Ind, and Coumadin Coumy. Vacant doodling, I suppose, but weird myths attend these drugs. I am down to two, of which one, Inderal, is somewhat undesirable as it raises your LDL cholesterol, even though it banishes hypertension and migraine and is a cardiological calmative. Other mysteries detain me now, most of all the finding that exercise can remedy the kind of diabetes I have—too much insulin coupled with weak response of the body cells to it. Exercise lowers the amount of insulin and also increases the body's sensitivity.

So on I go, wondering and blundering, a chronic pathic with a fidgety mind, anxious to be neither an

amateur cardiologist nor a professional patient. Daily
I peer out at a world full of carelessness, marred by
people who misuse computers and cancel all your
other reservations when the airline cancels a flight,
by anchorpersons who cannot write English or speak
it, buoying us up with the redundant bloat of such a
phrase as "during the course of the day." I consider
myself lucky to be in hands that falter little, machines
that do not lie, and drugs that by and large do not
change their personality. My best emblem has come
to be what Obeid did on my last visit. Ever courteous,
he ushered me into his office after the half-hour physical examination, during which he expressed plea-
surable surprise at how calm and steady my heart
was (one of its good days). After a while, he went
out and, when he returned, knocked at the closed
door. He *knocked on his own door*, paused, then
came back in. He not only knew how his patient felt
among the polished wood and the models of the
heart. The prefect of the beam that sees through you,
and interrogates you, had looked the other way for
once, giving my ghost a chance to collect its wits.

If you know any Latin, you will not be able to separate "cure" from *cura*, which sticks in my memory
thanks to King Alfred's translation of Pope Gregory
the Great's *Cura Pastoralis*, rendered as "Pastoral
Care." This, a tract instructing clergymen in their duties, became famous for King Alfred's preface: the

first significant prose in English. Even in Alfred's
hands, the notion of care shades into that of cure:
you cured souls by caring for them, you cared for
souls by curing them. In my dictionary, mesmerized
by what seems a religious duty to heal, I find such
wonders as Old Latin *coiraveront,* meaning they
cared for, and Paelignian *coisatens,* even Gothic
ushaista (needy). You cure a bad condition but heal
a breach. A curate is one in charge of soul-care. And
so on. The concept is inexhaustible and boundless,
but it doesn't seem yet to include caring for your own
soul. Norman Cousins wrote two books about caring
for himself (maybe curing himself) by laughter, an
activity that doubtless did him a lot of good. Plagued
by abscesses, I began to speak to the most recent of
them; I talked to my rear end, never aloud, but
frankly, extolling it and trying to soothe it, build it
up, giving it more than the time of day, certainly
more of a look-in than a conduit usually gets. Six
months later, I still had no abscesses, and I persist
with my fundamental oratory, sometimes administer-
ing a nursely pat where all that blood and pus had
poured. I told Obeid. "Anything that works," he said.
"Try everything." Yes, I thought, and then try it
again. Talking to one's body may indeed be part of
the *cura pastoralis* we have forgotten; feeding the bio
back is something only you can do for yourself. Spir-
itual isometrics, perhaps, keeping the talk of fistulas
and mangled sphincters at bay.

I was a sucker, therefore, for what the scholar-critic Mary Lynn Broe, a fellow diabetic, sent me: a clipping that reported research at the U.S. Department of Agriculture's Human Nutrition Research Center in Beltsville, Maryland. Cinnamon, I read, contains an unknown compound that may enormously increase the effectiveness of insulin. Indeed, of all the spices tested, cinnamon had a constant effect, boosting insulin activity in some experiments by almost twelve hundred percent. Oddly, although cinnamon contains chromium, a mineral associated with insulin effectiveness, other spices with more chromium produced less impressive results. There must be some other ingredient in cinnamon that works the trick. Biochemist Richard Anderson, who heads the Beltsville project, says his team is testing hundreds of different compounds, their hope being that one day cinnamon may let diabetics take less insulin and overweight diabetics, who often have insulin they can't use, begin to function normally. Anderson reports hearing from diabetics who have effected a marked improvement in their insulin activity by taking half a teaspoonful of cinnamon daily. Since reading this, I have become a cinnamonite, hoping to preclude my again having to take micronase—one of the insulin-receptor stimulators—which has been associated with some fatal heart problems and, in my own case, made my vision so blurry I couldn't read. Wouldn't *you* take half a teaspoon of cinnamon instead of a chemical that, as one guide to prescription drugs puts it, causes an increase in the death rate from heart disease ("A large study has shown" it)? Watch this space.

Only the other day, probing the word *diabetes* in the spirit of voodoo etymology (find its origin, exploit its heart), I realized that *diabetes* is Greek for compasses and siphon (the siphon part does not carry through into modern Greek, however). Surely this is an emblem for the ever-peeing diabetic who, in those ancient days, stood splay-legged in the performance and maybe walked that way all the time, just in case. Ever ready. The siphon is a related idea, perhaps: crossing over, as if you had your legs wide apart, for which motion the Greeks had a verb, *diabainein.* I'd like to know more about diabetes in Ancient Greece, more than Arteus (around A.D. 200), say, who coined the word: how it was regarded and dealt with. Did they realize how dangerous it was? What an ancient thing it is, even though the words for excessive thirst and excessive urination, *polydipsia* and *polyuria,* are ancient-looking modernisms. Knowing something this slight emboldens me, but not half as much as testing my blood sugar postprandially and finding it is 240, a vast improvement on the usual 350 and the 800s of a year ago. Now that we have our logo (the wide-legged piddler), can the cure be far behind?

LIVING WITH
A WILL

We have to learn, amidst this extreme reverence of life as a gift, the symbolic quality of lives spent, lives that have no quality left.

Big Two-Handed Engine

And so, in Pepysian mode (though to a longer rest than that envisioned in Samuel Pepys's formula "And so to bed"), I work my way around to contemplating the reaper, the grim one: the ultimate beneficiary of all this mess. The issue arises of dominating your own demise, your actual dying. It is not enough to accommodate yourself to the process, to ending defunct; you have to accommodate the process, at least, to you. Writing this last sentence, I feel old-fashioned, wondering where I have heard it all before: this get-with-it, spry, Spartan-sounding uplift. Surely it was some European hang-up. Instead of noble acquiescence, sock it to them, whoever the fates may be. Instead of being at the mercy of the big two-handed engine behind the cellar door—almost a capering Ko-kosori fire demon who wants to sink his teeth into me whenever I go down the cellar steps, thus fusing the monsters of my childhood with Hopi myth—you fight back and adapt the facts to your own conve-nience, drafting a so-called living will, a phrase whose ambiguity delights me: not only a document as active as if you were alive, but also a triumph of willpower, alas for its Nazi connotations. In other words, in this phrase your last will and testament supervises your final hours and your willpower lingers on, potent as ever, even while you are no longer in a condition to manage it.

Then the penny drops: this is existentialism, passé, perhaps, but emphatic in its blame and punch, its drive and pep. In a way, how American, America be-ing the country of all countries that lust emptorially after a few extra hours, days, of life, as if we had a right to it, as if it were worth enjoying, as if indeed life were a good and death was not, as if only life were appropriate for a human being whereas death was not. It is possible to be greedy and materialistic about life, squandering fortunes and skills to keep the damned thing going. Perhaps that is the honorable, the businesslike, the spunky thing to do, never going down until you utterly have to, smashed into nullity by a force you never comprehended. The weirdness of life, I have always thought, consists in the unfath-omable magic of birth juxtaposed with the humdrum

options available to us once born. The arrival is brilliant, the sequel limited. Anyway, with some sense of
an old friend on the doorstep and suasive still, I said
to myself:

Existentialism, one of our most hissing Isms, is
with us still. In the fifties and sixties, both a serious
philosophy and an almost hectic cult, it told us that
we alone are responsible for our lives: we have to
decide what we want to be and then be it. Its flavor
of heroic adventure recalled Horatio Alger and even
the old school of self-help. It was a philosophy per-
tinent not only to the American Dream, in which
yearning could prevail, but also to a Europe inventing
a dream of its own out of the ashes of World War
II. Above all, existentialism argued against passivity,
telling us to push, to take the blame, to be—above
all—energetic in designing ourselves. And its tonic,
rather puritanical message has hung around, reminding us that, in not the best of possible worlds, it's
possible to have the best of possible lives, and deaths
as well.

Existentialism had much to say about death, self-
inflicted or natural, little about dying, which is odd
inasmuch as we know a good deal about dying but
not much about death. Yet that is no odder than the
fact that we now apply to the act of dying much the
same energy we apply to living the good life. Never
have humans made such a minute study of dying's
fabric, almost as if dying were just another manipu-

lable disease. You *have* to catch it, but you may be able, if you develop a sharp enough legal and medical sense of it, to have one of its least expensive, least painful, and least humiliating versions. Such an on-slaught on dying amounts to more than antics in a condemned playground and reveals the human being as critic, fighter, and perfectionist to the end, tweak-ing and second-guessing not only a worsening con-dition but also the know-how and the whims of physicians and administrators, judges and relatives and friends. True, to know beforehand exactly what course one's terminal decline will take would require a prodigious feat of orchestrated prophecy performed by a team skilled in the ways of moribundity. But we have to try, even if only to have made a gesture to-ward not becoming dying's dupe as well as death's victim.

Consider the maze of fruitful legal conundrums the living will has created in the courts. We try to antic-ipate death to come, or rather part of the process that culminates in it, and hark what discord follows. In intention, the living will is more than a hopeful and stoical valedictory, a last fling at self-control; it pur-ports to be a stand free of ambiguities and exquisitely attuned to the conscience of survivors; yet in many instances it has proved incapable of exact interpre-tation and has had to be redefined by strangers. Courts of several kinds have questioned the use in living wills of such words as "reasonable" and "meaningful," even though such words remain definite enough for the discussion of everyday affairs. In the case of *Evans* v. *Bellevue Hospital* (1987), for instance, Tom Wirth, forty-seven, diagnosed as having AIDS Related Complex, executed a living will and medical power of attorney designating John Evans, his friend for twenty-two years, as his agent. On arrival at Bellevue, Wirth was in a stupor, unable to express himself, and suffering from toxoplasmosis (which, however, responds to antibiotics). Although, as the hospital argued, a living will is a valid instrument, in this case it failed to address the precise circumstances; indeed, to use the living will's own words, there was a "reasonable" chance that Wirth might "recover" or "regain a meaningful quality of life." The hospital also questioned Evans's capacity to construe the living will. Clearly, quibblers can always find something to quibble about, even in the most jesuitically refined wording, and the guardian, relative, or friend involved has to rely on someone's educated common sense to provide an appropriate and altruistic reading. So the hospital began life-sustaining treatment and Evans petitioned the court to have it stopped. After two weeks of antibiotics, Wirth had not recovered sufficiently to say what he wanted done, and the court sided with the hospital, maintaining that (1) Wirth could be expected to recover from the toxoplasmosis, (2) the living will was ambiguous, seeming to imply that, although Wirth

had ARC, he had envisioned life with it as having
"meaningful quality," and (3) Wirth might return to
a "cognitive" state ("cognitive" was not a word used
in his living will).

Evans argued that, when Wirth wrote "recover,"
he meant from ARC as well as from toxoplasmosis
and recalled Wirth's having *said* "he wanted to get
off this AIDS train." The court went further, citing
the "amorphous expression" of the living will and
urging that "great pains be taken by the drafters of
living wills to dispel the ambiguities which necessi-
tated this proceeding" (which itself is loosely put).
One wonders if even God Almighty, envisioning a
universe, had a sufficiently prescient blueprint to
hand. Clearly there is a language problem stemming
not so much from carelessness in wording or timing
as from ancient philosophical disputes never resolved:
the meaning of "meaning" haunts us still, and what
is reasonable still exercises the imagination. So long
as living wills invoke value judgments on lives lived
and lives ending, there is going to be dispute of an
almost classic character, and even the most determined, conscientious hair-splitter is going to be left
grappling with the problem of how someone no
longer communicable-with defined quality of life,
good or bad.

What seems to be lacking from such high-flown
discussion, all of it pedantic and chancy, is any
awareness of life as an opportunistic muddle from

atom to star. The mess of phenomena, or the chaos of them (to use a more fashionable term), is no tidier than the word hoard of ostensibly useful and agreed-on terms such as Wirth's blithely set down "reasonable" and "meaningful," or such contributions from the courts as *cognitive, proper, competent, incompetent,* if there be need for adjectives, and *privacy, battery, decision-making incapacity,* if there be need for nouns. If you add to this medley of legal and medical arcana such visions as that of the law being in an "unsettled" state (when there is no "compelling" evidence of the incompetent patient's wishes) and of the right to privacy as only a hint in the "penumbra" of the Bill of Rights, you long for another Moses fresh out of law school. It is no consolation to discover that, while courts wrangle with hospitals, many of the patients die anyway, as if chemistry had wearied of mind. We would like to think that, with some lexical virtuosity and a big dollop of enlightened goodwill, we could settle the matter before swooning away into brain death.

Even the most casual look at decisions handed down by courts as far apart as New Jersey and Colorado finds that hospitals and nursing homes favor surgery and life support, while courts go to sometimes considerable lengths to uphold living wills, even accepting the word of relatives or friends who manage to "remember" something the patient said, something tantamount or supplementary to a living will.

Each mystery favors the emblems of its own magic, though there are hospitals that deplore their gadgets and courts that deplore the law. At any rate, a rough-and-ready best-interest criterion seems to be emerging, predicated on attempts to divine the patient's sense of decorum. The New York State Supreme Court in 1987 listed eleven factors to be taken into account in arriving at a right-to-die decision, from the patient's age and life expectancy to statements made by the patient, the foreseeable quality of the patient's life, the views of people intimate with the patient, and pain—actually observing in the case of Sadie Weinstein, victim of two strokes and recommended for a mid-thigh amputation, that the initial onset of pain from nonamputation (treatable with palliatives) was preferable to the "pain and mutilation" of surgery.

It is as if, in courts across the land, judges were seeking to draft a charter or even a constitution for the dying, sifting from the morass of good intentions and righteous fiats the question: "What is it like to be you?" It would certainly be worth having a group of top-notch drafters drawn from the professions create a foolproof template, never mind how long, for the living will: one that could be agreed upon. Indeed, some forward-looking universities would be well advised to create chairs in Dying under the aegis of their programs in Biomedical Ethics.

There is not a single human being who, until the very end, is not obliged in some prescriptive way to

anticipate that end and its legal, medical, psycholog-
ical quality; so, if in our appetitive, competitive
country the government will not draft some Magna
Carta for the Moribund, then surely the nation's
intelligentsia—not its celebrities—should take the job
upon themselves with all the seriousness we claim to
apply to drugs. Or shall we have fifty years of high-
powered debate instead, while millions die untidily?

A Desert of Starched Linen

Seeking images, rather than judicial abstracts of the
dying process and the trouble it brings, we may well
turn to, and then reel away from, Frederick Wiseman's stunning film *Near Death*, aching for some set-
tled criterion that fleshes out the far from airy notion
that each of us is one's brother's or one's sister's
keeper. In Wiseman's six edited but uncontrived
hours of filming in the intensive care unit at Boston's
Beth Israel Hospital, doctors and nurses exhaust
themselves in the attempt not to initiate extreme
measures or prolong hopeless vegetating. Their minds
are very much on the difference between existence
(mere) and essence (the life of fully consummated
quality).

Surrounded by the machinery of pseudo reprieve,
they lament its efficacy, its inability to do for the
brain what it does for the heart. They argue among
themselves and with patients and relatives in favor of

disconnecting it or not using it at all, no doubt because almost all of the patients are terminally ill. Out of some preternatural sense of decorum perhaps unique to this hospital, they aim at emancipation painless and final: off the respirator, off the feeding tube, out of the bed, and into the home or the long steel drawers in the basement. They want to start the human race all over again, to start from scratch. What happens to the dying at the hands of both nature and medical technology distresses them. They spend much time extorting from relatives what should be done when the patient's life becomes so abstract and tiny a leftover it belongs in no human frame at all but in the beloved inventory of lost causes. We learn from this painful, epic movie that to cling to life, even as only a principle, an electrical squiggle, is normal; we know of nothing else. Yet we have to learn, amidst this extreme reverence of life as a gift, the symbolic quality of lives spent, lives that have no quality left. If your mind has vanished so much as to render you unaware of its loss, you had better stop clutching at what has already been taken away from you. We learn from *Near Death* that we too, like the poor souls in the footage, may eventually be reduced to a caricature much like a metronome ticking away, unaware of itself, in a desert of starched linen. For what? Out of some last-ditch stubbornness that says motion is life: better an induced mechanical fidget that we cannot appreciate, because we are no longer there, than a terminal silence we cannot appreciate either. The trouble is that, for the most part, you have to express yourself about it before you come to it, unless you have prodigious and faultless insight into how English fares in other people's brains.

More durable and dismaying than any such knowledge are the things the quiet-mannered, indefatigable Dr. Taylor says again and again. A master of compassionate redundancy, he tells his patients they can always change their minds, until they are no longer fit to make any decision at all. He is always having to ask the impossible of them and offering "to make your comfort our number one priority." We see living wills being redrafted by a potent scowl, or a flicker of the thumb, then erased by similar means, with the decision becoming more and more crucial as the patient slips away. People at their worst are having to make their worst decisions—and this applies to family as well as to patients. Taylor and his colleagues (most of them less politic) run a clearinghouse of will and decay. Pans clang. Phones ring. Nurses giggle. Mops swab the hallways. Machines beep, buzz, and suck. Wrapped like mummies, corpses await their gurney. "It's hard for someone not a doctor to decide," we hear, but they ask them anyway. "Doctors," we also hear, "can persuade people into just about anything."

They can in Holland, actually talking patients into

voluntary euthanasia for the good of society; heavy
propaganda for death has made elderly Dutch people
feel themselves a burden. Even in the U.S.A.,
"Granny Doe," as C. Everett Koop, former Surgeon
General, calls her, may run foul of the euthanasian
ethic fostered by Nazi Germany. The same fate, he
argues, could befall "a sidewalk screamer, an illegal,
undocumented alien, a mother of twelve and a grand-
mother of thirty-three, a nursing home resident with
Alzheimer's or a 'welfare queen,' an urban Indian, an
abandoned migrant worker." Right to life can also
mean the right to go on living or not, and it is not
so much delicate discernment as fully mobilized common sense that distinguishes between my finding my
own life no longer worthwhile and somebody else's
finding it thus before I do. One can see why some
states, such as Missouri, retain a vested interest in the
life of the individual, especially in view of the night-
mare conjured up by Dr. Koop; but one can also see
the wisdom in the New Jersey Supreme Court's re-
versal of the lower court by which it granted the relief
sought by Karen Ann Quinlan's father. "We think,"
the Court said in 1976, in its landmark decision,
"that the State's interest weakens and the individual's
right to privacy grows as the degree of bodily invasion increases and the prognosis dims. Ultimately
there comes a point at which the individual's rights
overcome the State interest."

An interested citizen may well wince at the vast

amount of information on this issue. Anyone devouring it would become wise without, perhaps, being able to translate such wisdom into sensible action. A host of comparable cases does not necessarily generate appropriate law, in Missouri or anywhere else. It makes sense to join the Society for the Right to Die, Concern for the Dying (the two may merge), and the Hemlock Society, and to study the *Hastings Center Report,* but it may make more sense to study, and perfect for one's own purposes, the Society for the Right to Die's specimen of a "New York Living Will." There are maps for study too, the most interesting of which reveals that South Dakota, Nebraska, Michigan, Ohio, New York, New Jersey, and Massachusetts have 1989 bills concerning living will legislation, while Pennsylvania and Kentucky have nothing, and the remainder all have laws already enacted. It depends where you live.

Terminal

In the end, one is in the predicament of both Isaiah Berlin's hedgehog (who knows one big thing) and his fox (who knows many little things). The big thing is that advance directives, as they are sometimes called, are more important than almost anything. The little things, in the form of court decisions and legislative bills, sprout up all around us. The pity is that the effort required to subsume the little things into the big one ends up scattered and fractured, almost lost in the very diversity of which Americans are proud. Perhaps only a country as small as Holland can achieve such homogeneousness as it has. Here one must put in several hours a week of study or miss such an enterprise as the Danforth-Moynihan "Patient Self-Determination Act of 1989," amending the Social Security Act, requiring hospitals and nursing homes to advise patients on arrival of their rights. Myself, I wonder about retirement communities into which you buy and are guaranteed appropriate care to the end. You lose your investment, of course, but you won't be wiped out by catastrophic costs. I wonder what happens if, at some point, you spurn the incessant care: do your heirs get some of your money back? After all, most of the big initial investment is for eventual nursing; what a luxury to sit comfortably, pondering such Last Things as the days roll by. A page or ten of immaculate English, allowing for all envisionable circumstances and lodged with the right people, may save much anguish as the courts and other institutions miscellaneously address themselves to problems long ago found insoluble by the best minds in the history of the world.

Not only do we make up our lives, and our selves, as we move along from birth to death; life improvises itself too, chemically and physically. Within the very concept "terminal" there are innumerable shadings for which there is no test. One of the arts of being human, in whatever era, has been to control ourselves and our lives even while having to live incoherently, as blank about tomorrow as about the purpose of life itself.

P O L A R

Q U I E T U S

Only a convenient shorthand for what was there,
mixing and surging as in a kaleidoscope.

Cantus Arcticus

There I go, leaping ahead of myself, but only as rational people are supposed to do in our advanced, initiative-ridden society. I shift from the immediate present to the eternal one, recalling something from my last visit to my mother. It was the last time I saw her. She lived five minutes' walk from my sister Sheila's home, even at ninety-four able to look after herself, more or less. Slow to get over my transatlantic jet lag, I had made myself late for lunch with my mother because, on the radio in my sister's house, playing to me with haphazard seductiveness, there had been all of a sudden a symphonic piece in which the classical orchestra mingled with the sounds of sea birds. Entranced, I had tried to work out who the composer might be, what nation, what school (Henry

Cowell, Carl Ruggles, William Bergsma, Roy Harris, Howard Hanson, Americans all), but I kept getting lost in the agreeable turmoil of the birds, of which there must have been a hundred thousand, from time to time drowning out the orchestra at random or when some musical artificer-general turned a knob. In a daze that made me both alert and nervy, I fought off the image of my waiting mother, the pianist who had cooked mint potatoes and fresh haddock for me, in order to concentrate on the reflex chorus of the birds as it wove its way among the pastoral music, mainly strings, as if the music's burden were precisely that, with such birds pouring forth, who needed symphonies?

I thus became ten, fifteen, thirty minutes late, at which point, no longer long-suffering, she phoned and asked if her clock was wrong. How could I be so late when I was only a few minutes' stroll away? I made some excuse while keeping my other ear on the music, awaiting the announcer's voice, unable to tell her I was standing her up for a piece of music, which she might almost have forgiven; but what I said to her had to do with health, and then she was all forbearing solicitude, as ever, and I wanted to be in real pain to pay myself out for being less than the son I should have been. I would hurry, I said, but she told me to take my time: the potatoes were on low, and the haddock was simmering in a white sauce. Look after yourself, she instructed me: "I don't want you out of breath when you arrive." She had never known of my illness, apart from the migraines and hives.

Why had I not told her I was listening to something, as she herself often did? Was I into compulsive secrecy? Perhaps I had thought it wouldn't be her kind of thing and was trying to spare her the affront of being kept waiting by something she would scoff at. Trying in vain to catch the syllables of an extremely foreign-sounding name, I wrote something down, then mentally gave myself the kick that energizes thought: In that country, the classical programs appear in all the newspapers, even in the tabloids, although there truncated to something such as "9.00 Elgar. 10. Bach. 11. Glinka." The paper that came to Sheila's house, however, gave all kinds of details. I dashed downstairs, almost falling over Bruno the dog, who slept in the hallway ready to devour anyone who rang the doorbell, and seized the newspaper, found the name: Einojuhani Rautavaara. Had any surname so many *a*'s in it? I could certainly not be telling her about this. She would scoff and remind me of the omnipresence, the intricate permanence, of Beethoven. What I had heard, almost overheard, had been *Cantus Arcticus,* played by Pekkanen and the Klemetti Institute Symphony Orchestra. The music, perhaps because of the stress set up in me by making Mother wait, had delivered me to a far-distant land I now knew was Finland, whether Arctic or not, a country where one radio station broadcast in Latin. Here was music a devout alchemist might grow to love, simply for its unclassified, harum-scarum quality. It was the saddest music I had heard in months, though I rejoiced because it made me decide between bird and viola.

I said goodbye to Bruno, strolled gently through the summer fug of Rutlandshire, past the six-foot-high bulrushes that grew in someone's utterly kempt garden, turned left at the phone box, crossed the empty main street of the village, and walked uphill past the post office, closed for the afternoon because this was Wednesday Early Closing. It was here that I usually stocked up for her on iced Popsicles, fizzy drinks, and sugar jellies. Arrived at last, I squeezed her frail body against mine, late but forgiven and overwhelmingly moved because I knew she was a much finer human than I was, though not above a few querulous questions about the afterlife, angels, and heaven. My mind winced away sideways to find some counterpoint to the sweet banality of chewing haddock in white sauce, but found, however, no procession of Arctic birds, no illuminated skeleton beginning its dance in the cave of horrors, but something subtler, less easy: another music altogether. Watching my mother's face as it tautened, relaxed, then readdressed itself had been like hearing a late Beethoven quartet as it went from wry, somewhat mutinous, euphoric resignation to bold, somewhat

mutinous, euphoric resignation, to bold, somewhat humbled, euphoric resignation, to bold, somewhat humbled, sedate resignation, to bold, somewhat
humbled, sedate restiveness, only to begin again with
the emotions varying two or three at a time while I
racked my brains to freeze in words the exact, complete spectrum of feeling that leapt out of a certain
phrase I called—until then—the polar quietus. It was
more intricate than that, of course, and calling it that,
as I repeatedly had, was only a convenient shorthand
for what was there, mixing and surging as in a
kaleidoscope:

> humility
> spleen
> shy acquiescence
> tear-in-the-eye doggedness
> tender indecisiveness
> brio
> patrician ruefulness
> domineering modesty
> hubris.

On I had gone, over the years, inspired by the superb
musician that she was, to pin down Beethoven in the
manner of the novelist. Impossible. The chore would
never end; there would always be shadings within
shadings within shadings. I would never be able to
trap in words the exact woof of Beethoven or anyone

else: nothing overstated, nothing extraneous, nothing left out, of course. Only a musician, such as I was not, could read it.

So with her face: seamed and sunken, indeed ravaged, yet tinctured with an elfin, haughtily playful quality she had always had and which made her so approachable and popular. The instant she entered a room, people who had no idea who she was began gravitating to her side, to ask her advice, to see how she was getting on. I considered this invitingness of hers a variant on her platform manner, which began mild and diffident but fast turned flamboyant and keen. She found this aspect of her nature amusing, and was even more amused when I told her that, in airports, all I had to do was sit down, and various unattached-looking children would begin to approach me to watch, to play, to smile, no doubt recognizing one of themselves or detecting someone bizarre from light-years away.

A Compact Disc

So, dumbfounded and self-condemned by mere reverie, I told her about the birds, half wondering if she would connect them with the lateness of my arrival, ironically saying that music had come between us once again (I having gone to words instead of notes). Instead she asked about the fish, having set the notion of lateness lolling in the empyrean of things best left

unsaid. How did I like the haddock? I began to wonder about the sentient birds, the sentient orchestra (or
the sentient composer?), even as she seemed pointedly
to ignore the birds, at whose exploitability I wondered. They had no control over serious composers
except as inspiration: Respighi, Messiaen, and now
this Finn, whose evocation of brooding wilderness
had opened up my vitals and flummoxed my heart.

"Thousands of swans," I told her, "but there were
lighter birds too. I think they tampered with some of
the calls, making them lower, but I remember best
how the music seemed to swoon in the presence of
them all and nearly gave up the ghost, as if over-
whelmed or outfaced. Odd how the birds didn't seem
to yield an inch of ground to the orchestra, which of
course they could not hear. Wouldn't it have been
better to play 'cantus' music to the birds and record
the result? Leaving it as it is makes the birds an absolute and the 'cantus' the only protean thing. Of
course."

"Was anyone," she asked, "conducting the birds?"
Had she said that with an astute glower? My stomach
made the sound of a baby puma. I felt as awkward
as when I had had to crack tablets of Quinaglute in
half—they never broke evenly. It was all right to tell
her about Rautavaara; she jumped right at the idea
and became a player. My illness, which she would
orchestrate in a trice, would have to remain secret.

"What a wonderful idea," I said. "No, the birds

were just doing their own thing when they recorded them. I suppose." I almost blushed, evicted from reverie.

"Then they had to take potluck," she said. "It would just be bird noise, then. *Sounds*." She sometimes took the wrong pills; she took them all wrong, but she seemed to survive them so long as they all churned around inside her. I told her about Rautavaara's music instead of confiding to her about my illness. I bought a compact disc of *Cantus Arcticus*, which my mother never heard. Nor have I played it. Dumb badge or enigmatic changeling of my illness, it will go with me sealed for the rest of my days.

SEEING STARS

I have just been peering at a sketch, made in 1870 by a British physician, Hubert Airy, of the so-called fortification illusions familiar to migraine subjects: concentric bright strata, like saw-toothed horseshoes, which expand in concert across the visual field. From his own and his father's experience, Airy concluded that the visual displays characteristic of migraine evince the structure of the brain itself, even proposing that, as spontaneous perceptions, they amounted to a portrait of actual processes in the brain. So what you "see" during an attack is not only, to some extent, what is there before your eyes, but also what is behind them: you're watching not only how you mis-see, but, in a rudimentary way, also regions of the brain that receive data directly from the eyes. I mean individual neurons whose only function is to respond, say, to lines of a certain length at such and such an angle: feature-detectors rather like sentries, programmed to notice such things as slashes or hyphens and nothing else. Sometimes, I understand, these detectors activate themselves spontaneously, say when we are under pressures that somehow reduce blood flow, or when local ionic balance has been upset; and it is this activity we are perceiving when assorted scintillant bars and corners swim into view and add up to what resembles a plan view of pretechnological fortifications (zigzag mound or moated maze).

In my own experience, the optical upset precedes the headache by several hours, taking half an hour or so to reach a maximum that can last for over an hour. The first thing is a twinkling blind spot just on the visual field's periphery and fringed with brilliants. Soon the spot increases, the fringe becomes a serrated arc of matchsticks dabbed red, orange, or yellow at the ends, which seems to wheel or roll in the presence of parallel arcs larger or smaller; then the one arc disappears, another shows up, and the entire reflexive process—of undizzily observing dizziness—starts over, with occasional flashes of cobalt or kingfisher blue as it redevelops its face, like a map of an electrical field radiating from a point in the cerebral cortex. According to the neuropsychologist K. S. Lashley, from the evidence of *his* own migraines, the propagation rate is about an eighth of an inch per minute, even though the larger arcs appear to move faster. Slow enough to be described to an accomplice, or even to be sketched if you attend exactly and draw on portions of paper that match unoccluded regions of sight, these phenomena are nonetheless tricky to hold in the mind: they dazzle, wobble, come simply and complicatedly go, refulgent protean flakes which remind me of Heisenberg's dictum that "by its intervention science alters and refashions the object of its investigation. In other words, method and object can no longer be separated." To go through the motions of looking closely changes somewhat the display in the part of the brain you're viewing: the decision to examine seems to shunt the cortical movie in a new direction or move a certain arc out of focus. You feel like the telescopist tracking stars only three seconds of arc apart without some kind of electrically driven clock.

Even so, it is possible to identify arcs fringed with corporal's stripes, the outside chevrons flashing alternately with the inner at an oscillation rate of something like five cycles per second. The result is a motion variously described as boiling, rolling, or metronomic, akin in my own ocular experience to the formation drill (say northeast to west to east to north) performed on my retinas by little congeries of cells when I close my eyes against the sun. When the chevrons number as many as (I think) ten, intact or broken and impacted, to a unit, like overcrowded broken chromosomes, the visual display becomes a reeling swarm. Such is the full-spate migraine, the main difference between early and mature arcs being that between horseshoe and sausage shapes, the main difference between the simple and the complex hatchings being that, with the former, you can see the inner ones switch off while the outer ones light up, and vice versa, whereas, with the latter, you can't: with almost a dozen to watch, component and wave become indistinguishable as light shuttles across the grid, renewing itself fluidly, rippling as the display cants clockwise or counter-. Between the individual lines, gorgeous although dismembered bolts of color appear, and I, confined to my private chromosphere, egotistically magnify them into stellar presences: the salvia red of Betelgeuse and Antares, indicating titanium oxide at five and a half thousand degrees Fahrenheit; the peachy orange of Arcturus and Aldebaran, where metals predominate over hydrogen; the true yellow of our sun, or triple Capella the Goat, both highly metallic; the yellowish pus-white of Canopus in Carina, index to decreasing hydrogen; the ermine white of Sirius, the brightest star of all, where hydrogen reigns; the blue white of Rigel and Spica, sign of strong natural helium; the even bluer white of Iota Orionis, in Orion's sword, where the gases are strongly ionized at a temperature exceeding sixty thousand F. I thus staged in my visual cockpit exotic spectra all the way from simple compounds' badges to emblems of excited or ionized atoms: like campaign ribbons from the constant war between mineral and heat, inertia and hysteria; a compensatory mind game for a self-obstructing hothead whose blood supply's gone temporarily askew. For reasons I do not know, however, my spectra held more red-hot and blue-hot than yellow-hot bands, an underpresented middle spectrum that matches the experiences of other migraineurs, and we agree on the absence, relative or total, of green, a color little seen in the star classification chart itself. I did not loosely analogize my inward show as therefore rich in titanium oxide and ionized gases; after all, my cortex doesn't happen to be any number of light-years away or however many thousand degrees hot; but the conceit was beguiling, especially when I had to witness unsolicited lightnings, in the course of which both eyes looked backward into the inventive pith of the brain itself.

Behind the teeth of superimposed circular saws of varying diameters, there are the blades, blanks of blindness into which the sketcher's pencil tip vanishes, only to be made to reappear by a slight tug. Astronautically speaking, this is the terminator, demarking a temporary unknown region that behaves very oddly indeed, making exceptions to its own occlusions (maybe the domestic equivalent of the anything-goes in the vicinity of a black hole's so-called absolute event horizon). For example: if I am not aware that I am failing to see something that is there, in the zone of blindness, I may not detect the zone at all, partly because (oh, neuronal bag of tricks!) it's been filled in by another bit of the brain. If, say, you happen to look at a TV screen, it may

disappear in whole or in part, only to be replaced by
the wall behind it, while the stand it squats on remains visible throughout. Such vicarious self-help by
the brain evokes some of the transferences of function
that brain-damaged people have achieved and sug-
gests cerebral versatilities as yet unexplained. Surely,
though, memory does some of this filling in, even on
the strength of only a few seconds' acquaintance with
the furniture of a particular room. Surely, too, non-
visual neurons stand in for those that, as it were, are
playing Narcissus at the eyes' expense, against banks
of colored clouds: lenticular, bubble, mushroom,
pear, and many other shapes. The compensations, py-
rotechnical or merely motoric, are many, though I
doubt if they correspond exactly to what local co-
gnoscenti credit you with as you float by in dark
glasses, badge of the addict. I used to smile at my
pseudo status and devote a blink of thanks to whatever power gave me trips I never wanted. Odd: dark
glasses got me a reputation for LSD and, more recently, the redness of my eyes one for grass. Unde-
served, both; I never wandered in those heady realms;
I sought some grail in alcohol instead.

From such amateur self-perceptions as these, it is
possible to hunt the neuron down to its pulpy lair
and uncover the hexagonal honeycomb of its polis;
but that is a chore requiring fine instruments and a
readiness to tongue such lumps as "the neural sub-
strate of the cortex's being organized into discrete el-

ements at a level at or above that of individual
neurons." My kind of migraine nods head deferen-
tially at the expert's newfangled, exact *trouvailles* and
dwells instead on how, after a bout, the scalp is painful to touch, often for a day or two, while the headache succumbs to a pellet of Darvon, which gets you
not so much sleepwalking as sleepsitting, bemusedly
wondering if the cortical Fourth of July—a display in
the brain and not the result of light's entering the
eye—happened at all. A radiant abstract, of plunging
motes and Mount Palomar telescopic hues, remains,
half tempting you to wish the next bout nearer, half
daunting because it threatens eventual monopoly by
a photophobia whose gear includes double-thick Po-
laroids, black silk eye masks, a self-imposed ban on
reading, semipanic at the lightest snowfall, even the
blanched disk of a cheesecake, and the closer-
nurtured hunch that some Lilliputian solar flare has
your name on it and you have an appointment with
blindness. Calmer, you register a private thank you
for the silent movie of your brain eyeing itself (much
perhaps as Homo sapiens intones a grace for knowing that he knows he can think), and all those crab-
wise antic dances of the colors—the schottische of
the cerebral stars as they swing around some un-
charted epicenter, the quadrille done by minor photic
components, the smooth-run conga joined by bands
of darkness linking up as they move ever outward—
seem a boon, at least more a benighted privilege than

an affliction: a temporary and exalting mishap not
worth whipping up into a whole *tsimmes*.

Goneril with a White Beard

Or so I have come to believe after five decades,
amounting to no more than six hundred visitations
by this intracranial Phoebus, complete with rockets,
Catherine wheels, and Roman candles. All those star
shells, exploding silently above a distant war front an
inch behind my eyes, remind me in the long run of
my statistical congeners: ten percent of the race has
to endure migraine headaches from time to time (a
similar percentage to that for alcoholics), and about
half of those headaches involve visual areas of the
brain. Twenty-five million Americans is a burly sodality, and of course migraineurs have banded together worldwide; there are clinics, much relief: you
feel less one of the walking wounded, rather one who
has seen the lightning and found it testily lyrical, not
bad for a corps de ballet mustering one hundred bil-
lion brain cells powered at most, in toto, by twenty-
five watts, one joule per second. Unprovoked by this
half holiday, I might never, in fictional texts, have
had so much fun in addressing myself to the egotistic
last surviving brain cell of William Shakespeare on
the day of his death, to Manfred Vibber the physicist
(a Nobel laureate who, after staring at the sun, pre-

posterously begins to see by polarized light), or to
Leonardo da Vinci, mesmerizing himself into the
twentieth century, near closing time, by staring at the
melanic splotch of a black hole. The valiant editors
who bought these stories purchased a snippet of my
private life as well, a few shows from my most esoteric amphitheater, where there is no applause, no
script, but a cast of millions and lighting equal to an
overhead fluorescent lamp. Full of gratitude, I rather
miss the old attacks, and my imaginative counterpoint intended to fend them off: sack and fall of the
main installation, the head, the fissure of Rolando
choked with corpses, both hippocampi flying the
black flag of the eternal killjoy foe, the brain stem
itself a single corm of dead celery, vanadium white
and toadstool brown, the eyes uselessly globose, the
whole assembly less useful than the electrode-loaded
brain of a rhesus monkey.

Against a gratitude so long postponed, I have no
defense. In ham-fisted ways, I managed to halt attacks in twenty minutes, a handy bit of cerebral mil-
itarism, though with a pang for all the canceled
coronal discharges (a Saint Elmo's fire, or corposant,
of the mind), the petty visual fizz, the coruscating lu-
nettes, all the way from rosy-pink silicate to the dark
blue-black of the king mackerel. Stop, light show: I
need to see my notes. Still the mildly nauseating euphoria that is the show's herald, but curb the show
long before its white-spiked haloes egg me on. All, in

quizzical or superstitious moments, I find to wonder at—ferreting about for a Philoctetian curse minus the wound's reek—is my being in part left-handed (or a shifting sinistral), about which I dumbly interrogate the deep dent in my left skull (twin to the one in my mother's and about which she knew nothing).

No hallucinogens needed, says my private sign: migraine itself has taken me far afield, sent me on a galactic and chromatic wild-goose chase whose back-handed bonus has been spectral analogies beyond price, sometimes even beyond words. Has any scientific nonprofessional felt a telescope, a microscope, so natural a prolongation of his gratis brain? Far and near things have pavanned before organs whose limbering-up exercises I have had to eye. Head's silky inscape has repeatedly come clean, showed off its paces under the guidance of Count Volta, eponym of the volt. More than once I have been edgily perturbed, not by inconvenience or frustration, but by being my instrument's slave. Slightly at risk, only a modicum the victim, and considerably balked, I have still been able to marvel at the flawed ziggurat patterns of naked energy behind my eyes (inducing just a touch of backstage fright), as well as at the initial exhilaration, when you feel like a Greek triskelion: three-armed, with a grinning, tongue-out, solar face where the arms join. Your eyes, observers tell, glisten copiously during a bout, and afterward a dark ring forms under each of them, evoking the underlined eyes of the fish called Butter Hamlet, suggestive of debauchery limited, in fact, to spasms of involuntary blinking. The rest is private, but, in this self-studying case, not even epiphanic: no intuition of religious mystery accompanies the symptoms, only a bargain sense of awe, as if a druid had happened upon a flashlight during a thunderstorm at Stonehenge. No big catechism, no pat vision: just a ravishing nuisance, as far from nirvana as from Alpha Centauri. I complain about it but, in the end, rate it a plus.

A diary entry of many years ago, scrawled during an attack, reminds me of more wretched, apocalyptic feelings I then had. You become inured, though never indifferent, especially to the remote possibility, evoked by that diary, of having an attack begin while actually writing this down. As it happens, neither the theme nor the perusal of my old on-the-spot notation, nor the bulb's brightness on the yellow pad or the white typing paper, has sparked things off: my nuisance is still captain of its fate, and I am content to part from it thus, with a cordial transcription:

"Comes now the first renegade pinpoint of light, a tiny triangle multicolored and southwest in my field of vision, inviting and warning, extending itself so fast I almost sneeze as if I am looking at the sun. An arc of glittering triangles spreads northeast, then spins round through all remaining points of the optical compass and thickens up into a private nebula that now blots out most of the things I know are there, now lets up on the left (some of the room is still there), now on the right (and that part of the room is there too), then lets up nowhere at all, and I am at the center of a maelstrom that is all reeling, spinning brilliants, most of them still triangular although a few race across the nebula like misbehaving particles. It is like being the victim of a melting rainbow. It is the optic nerve saying, I will not serve.

"I write this without looking, as if taking notes at a lecture, the speaker's face being one you cannot look away from. Now I *know* there are silver ores in my head. I think ancient codes are being decoded behind my eyes, buzzes and blurts of light whose grammar is that of space curving in whatever space curves in. I'd quote, if I could, that same old text, not because it brings comfort, but because it's better to have a parallel than not, as the Mercator map projections say to one another in the navigators' cupboards aboard ships."